A Librarian's Guide to ISO Standards for Information Governance, Privacy, and Security

A Librarian's Guide to ISO Standards for Information Governance, Privacy, and Security

Phyllis L. Elin and Max Rapaport

BEP

BUSINESS EXPERT PRESS

Leader in applied, concise business books

A Librarian's Guide to ISO Standards for Information Governance, Privacy, and Security

First published in 2023 by
Business Expert Press, LLC
222 East 46th Street, New York, NY 10017
www.businessexpertpress.com

ISBN-13: 978-1-63742-545-9 (paperback)
ISBN-13: 978-1-63742-546-6 (e-book)

Business Expert Press Business Law and Corporate Risk Management Collection

First edition: 2023

10 9 8 7 6 5 4 3 2 1

Description

In the digital age, librarians and archival professionals play a crucial role in safeguarding the world's knowledge. *A Librarian's Guide to ISO Standards for Information Governance, Privacy, and Security* is a curated resource for librarians, presenting core ISO standards related to information governance, data privacy, and security.

The book provides detailed summaries of these standards, along with case studies and advice on applying them in the modern digital age. It empowers library staff and patrons to prioritize data security and privacy, ensuring trust and confidentiality in their services.

The purpose is to demystify critical standards related to information security and records management privacy information management for the modern librarian and archival professional.

Inside, you will find detailed summaries of the core ISO standards, descriptions, and case studies illustrating how these standards can apply to librarians in the modern digital age, advice on how to cultivate a culture of data security, and privacy awareness among library staff and patrons.

Keywords

librarians; ISO standards; ISO 27701; ISO 15489; information governance; privacy; security; information management; information governance by design; library management; data protection; risk assessment; information security; compliance; personally identifiable information; personal data; information systems; legal research; data subject rights; risk management

Contents

Introduction

I have been a global consultant in the field of information governance (IG) and compliance for over 40 years. During that time, the metamorphosis of records management to IG has given me a somewhat unique perspective. My education began in Cincinnati, Ohio, in the 1970s where, along with a small group of women, I was schooled in the tenets of best practices for records and information management (RIM). My professors were formidable women who cut their teeth working for the U.S. Federal Government during World War II. So, eager for a career as a perpetual student, and combining my curiosity with my admiration, the teaching methods of my two mentors played beautifully into my scholarly inclinations.

Though RIM basics were not in my wheelhouse as an English major and political science minor, as the training began, it immediately appealed to my sense of reason and organization. RIM spoke to me. I was enthralled by it. As I absorbed these learning sessions, I felt the same academic excitement as I did for my classes at New York University. In addition to the building blocks of my education, I also nurtured traits of patience, meticulousness, and logic. These were paramount to this career path, and I was encouraged in believing that I possessed these skills.

My IG and compliance career has taken me to many countries and continents, all of which, for better or worse, treat RIM at least a little differently. My journeys have also allowed me to see and understand many organizations in most vertical markets and jurisdictions. I interviewed subject matters experts (SMEs) in all functional areas as to their record-keeping requirements, workflow perils and pitfalls, and many a parade of horribles.

With the expansion of technology and governance, our industry has often changed very dramatically and abruptly. The shift in data privacy rules and regulations is just the most recent example. Still, there are standards and best practices which transcend the sudden vicissitudes of the day, and these more enduring, universal principles will be the focus of this volume.

That said, the foundation of my observations generally begins with ISO 15489, established in 2001 as the first globally recognized requirement for RIM. And thus, the workflows will more or less adhere to the following protocol: capture; check; record; consolidate and review; and act; coupled with accountability, transparency, integrity, protection, compliance, accessibility, retention, and disposition. We will also touch on archives management and the two principles of providence and original order.

Thereafter, I will cover a number of general subject areas from the perspective of people, process, and technology. These areas will include, inter alia, strategic alignment, management principles, continuous improvement, organizational continuity, metrics, and risk and operations management.

Finally, we will take a deeper look at the principles and implications of IG as they pertain to libraries. The first portion of this section will focus on international standards applicable to libraries in both the United States and internationally and the second part will shift toward a discussion of specific interest topics applicable to libraries, as a whole. This portion of the book was written by my collaborator, Max Rapaport, an attorney with expertise in the areas of records management and data privacy.

CHAPTER 1

What Is Information Governance?

As its name implies, information governance (IG) is a comprehensive strategy for managing an enterprise's people, process, and technology, with an emphasis on risk, legal compliance, information management, and business intelligence. IG also subsumes a number of disciplines such as e-discovery, data privacy, big data, architecture, operations, organizational continuity, and audit.

Broadly defined, IG includes the management of information within an organization or enterprise. It includes a broad range of policies, procedures, and technology used to manage the life cycle of information, from creation to disposal. Its central purpose is to ensure that information is managed in a way that supports an entity's goals and objectives, while also complying with legal and regulatory requirements. These goals include promoting regulatory compliance, helping employees find the "right information at the right time," ensuring the disposal of unneeded or duplicate data, and helping entities to ensure that the right versions of documents are preserved.

One widely accepted definition of IG comes from the Sedona Conference, a nonprofit organization dedicated to the advanced study of law and policy in areas of antitrust law, complex litigation, and intellectual property rights. Unfortunately, like many definitions for IG, the Sedona Conference couches the term in somewhat academic language. Specifically, the Sedona Conference defines IG as "an organization's coordinated, interdisciplinary approach to satisfying information compliance requirements and managing information risks while optimizing information value."[1] This definition highlights the need for IG to be a cross-functional effort that involves various stakeholders across an organization.

More importantly, perhaps, the Sedona Conference established a set of principles for IG, known as the Sedona Principles.[2] These principles provide guidance to organizations on how to develop and implement effective IG programs. The principles are as follows:

- Organizations should have a sound and reasonable basis for their IG policies.
- IG policies should be consistent with the organization's legal obligations, industry standards, and business objectives.
- IG policies should be designed to minimize the risks and costs associated with the preservation and disclosure of electronically stored information.
- Organizations should identify and manage information in a timely and efficient manner, taking into account the nature of the information and the needs of the organization.
- Organizations should have an ongoing process for monitoring and improving their IG policies and procedures.
- Organizations should implement policies and procedures to ensure that the information they collect, use, and disclose is accurate, complete, and up-to-date.
- Organizations should implement appropriate security measures to protect information from unauthorized access, use, disclosure, alteration, or destruction.
- Organizations should implement policies and procedures to ensure that information is disposed of in a timely and secure manner when it is no longer needed.

Another definition of IG comes from Gartner, a leading research and advisory company. Gartner defines IG as "the specification of decision rights and an accountability framework to ensure appropriate behavior in the valuation, creation, storage, use, archiving, and deletion

---

[1] https://thesedonaconference.org/sites/default/files/publications/Commentary%20on%20Information%20Governance_0.pdf.
[2] Id.

of information."[3] This definition highlights the importance of assigning responsibility and accountability for managing information throughout its life cycle.

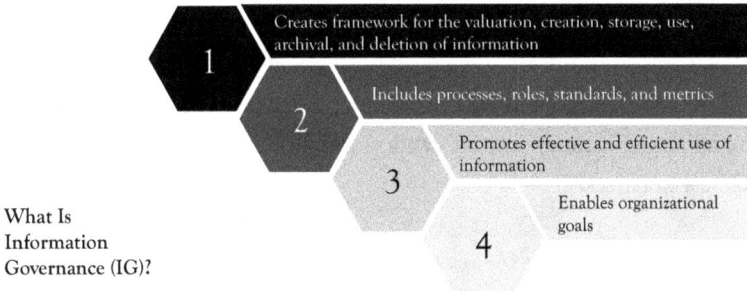

What Is Information Governance (IG)?

1 — Creates framework for the valuation, creation, storage, use, archival, and deletion of information

2 — Includes processes, roles, standards, and metrics

3 — Promotes effective and efficient use of information

4 — Enables organizational goals

Source: Gartner

But, that is not all…

- The International Organization for Standardization (ISO) defines IG as "the system of controls, policies, procedures, and technologies used to manage information throughout its life cycle, from creation to disposal, in order to minimize risk, ensure compliance with legal and regulatory requirements, and maximize value."[4]
- The Healthcare Information and Management Systems Society (HIMSS) defines IG in the health care context as "a strategic approach to managing enterprise information assets that enables an organization to support its business objectives, maximize its value, minimize its risks, and ensure its compliance."[5]
- The Association for Information and Image Management (AIIM) defines IG as "the activities and technologies that organizations employ to maximize the value of their information while minimizing associated risks and costs."[6]

---

[3] www.gartner.com/en/information-technology/glossary/information-governance.

[4] www.iso.org/obp/ui/#iso:std:iso:24143:ed-1:v1:en.

[5] www.himss.org/resources/himss-public-policy-principles.

[6] https://armacanada.org/information-governance-vs-data-governance-whats-the-difference-and-why-does-it-matter/.

- The Electronic Discovery Reference Model (EDRM) defines IG as "the process of creating, implementing, and enforcing policies and procedures to manage information assets in order to meet legal, regulatory, and business requirements."[7]

When communicating the need for IG, however, we have often found it to be more effective to rely on simpler, nonacademic language and on the net organizational impact of adopting defensible and understandable IG best practices.

How We (Don't) Need to Talk About IG

Professor-speak

We should not "naively treat filmic evidence as a transparent window revealing the whole truth, as a presentation of unambiguous reality." (article about amusement park liability)

Instead, say:

*Don't trust film of the accident.
It's not always accurate.*

Nearly every definition of IG from the Big 4, to ARMA, to the Sedona Conference uses professor-speak...

Instead...

What Is Information Governance?

A set of tools that...

- Reduces data costs
- Improves legal compliance
- Protects important records
- Helps employees find their records faster

7 https://edrm.net/resources/frameworks-and-standards/information-governance-reference-model/.

CHAPTER 2

What Questions Does Information Governance Help to Answer?

Information governance best practices help research libraries and other organizations to identify, manage, and protect their important data throughout all phases of their life cycle. Based on our experience, this understanding can be broken down into three general categories:

1. *Knowing what information they need*: Information governance helps research libraries to identify the types of information they need to operate effectively. One of the critical elements of this process is the inventory data assets, which include both the automated and the manual review of structured and unstructured data. This review can help librarians to make informed decisions about where to focus their data management efforts and prioritize their information management initiatives. In a typical use case, the librarian would conduct a data inventory of the entity's collections, including its physical and digital assets, to determine which resources are most important to the library's mission and which should be deprioritized or deselected based on either an absence of need or the requirements of a retention schedule (or privacy laws). When conducted properly, the overall result is generally an optimization of the use of the library's resources and a measurable record showing that the library is investing its time and budget wisely.

2. *Understanding how to use information*: Once an entity has identified which data assets are the most critical, information governance best practices can be harnessed to help further define how that information should be used. This definition includes creating policies around

data access, usage, and sharing, as well as establishing rules around retention, archiving, and disposal, and guidelines around data use. The result is that the enterprise can ensure that its information is being used in a way that aligns with its strategic objectives and complies with applicable laws, regulations, and industry standards. An example of this process is a case where the research librarian cooperates with other staff to establish policies and procedures governing data retention and disposal. This process generally includes identifying which types of data should be archived or preserved and which can be deleted or destroyed (and how the data should be destroyed). The end result is that the librarian will play a key role in helping the library to optimize the use of storage resources and to ensure that the library is only retaining data that is truly valuable and necessary for its operations.

3. *Allocating responsibility for information management*: Information governance can also help libraries to define clear roles and responsibilities around their data ownership, management, and protection. This type of enterprisewide accountability helps to ensure that all the relevant personnel understand their role in managing and protecting the library's critical information assets. In addition, it helps libraries to identify the right data stewards and custodians who should be responsible for managing specific data assets, establish clear policies governing data access and usage, and enforce and promote sound data management standards through regular training and education. An example of this role is a research librarian, who could work with the library's legal team to ensure that the library is compliance monitoring, to promote compliance with applicable laws and regulations governing data management and privacy that is bolstered by ongoing training and education for library staff around best practices for data handling.

CHAPTER 3

Why Is Information Governance Important to Librarians and Other Knowledge Workers?

The IFLA Code of Ethics for Librarians and other Information Workers[1] sets forth various information governance-centric goals. Foremost among these goals are:

- The duties of librarians and information workers to improve transparency
- The obligation to continually develop the knowledge and skills required for their profession
- The commitment to support optimal recording and representation of information and to provide access to it[2]
- The duty to provide access to information and to ensure universal access to information (closely aligned with transparency)
- The duty to present content in a way that allows an autonomous user to find the information he or she needs (aligned with the idea of information integrity or ensuring that the correct information is delivered at the correct time)

---

[1] Copy of IFLA Code of Ethics for Librarians and other Information Workers (long version).

[2] The basis for this goal is described in the United Nations Universal Declaration of Human Rights (1948), which establishes a universal duty to recognize and acknowledge the humanity of others and to respect their rights, including the freedom of opinion, expression, and access to information.

- The duty to protect personal data
- The duty to support government information transparency
  initiatives

While these goals do not represent the full spectrum of information governance priorities, it is clear that librarians and knowledge workers operating on both public and private levels are critical to the development of information quality and transparency and, of course, to privacy laws, all of which form part of the fabric of information governance.

CHAPTER 4

Good Information Governance Versus Bad Information Governance

In the context of research library management, poor information governance in a research library that manages texts and documents from multiple countries manifests in a variety of ways. These include:

- *Inconsistent metadata*: Metadata is essential to manage and discover library resources effectively. Poor information governance practices by research librarians include the use of inconsistent, inaccurate, or incomplete metadata, which can make it difficult to find relevant materials, increased data search times, and mistakes related to version control.
- *Duplication of effort*: When information is not managed effectively, research librarians will need to duplicate routine tasks such as cataloging, indexing, and storing information. This leads to unnecessary costs and, as with metadata, increased mistakes.
- *Lack of standardization*: One of the hallmarks of good information governance practices is standardization across an enterprise's departments or divisions Poor information governance practices often result in a lack of standardization across collections, which can make it difficult to compare and analyze information across multiple sources and to poor quality control.
- *Limited access*: If information is not managed properly, it can be challenging to grant appropriate access to researchers, scholars, and the public, which can result in delays, frustration, and additional negative research impacts.

- *Inadequate security*: Research libraries often manage sensitive or confidential information, and research librarians are often the ultimate parties responsible for ensuring that appropriate security measures are in place. Poor information governance protocols can lead to inadequate security controls, leaving data vulnerable to unauthorized access, theft, or other threats.
- *Poor preservation*: Research librarians often handle sensitive and easily degradable collections. Poor information governance may lead to a lack of proper preservation (e.g., temperature controls), which can result in materials deteriorating or becoming obsolete.
- *Inefficient workflows*: Inadequate information governance can lead to inefficient workflows that can impact productivity and delay research outcomes.
- *Excess storage*: One of the core elements of a good information governance practice is reduced storage space. Research libraries that fail to dispose of redundant, obsolete, and trivial data and other materials that have a low business or academic value face both high online storage costs and wasted physical space.

Conversely, research libraries that have strong information governance protocols in place tend to exhibit the traits given in the figure.

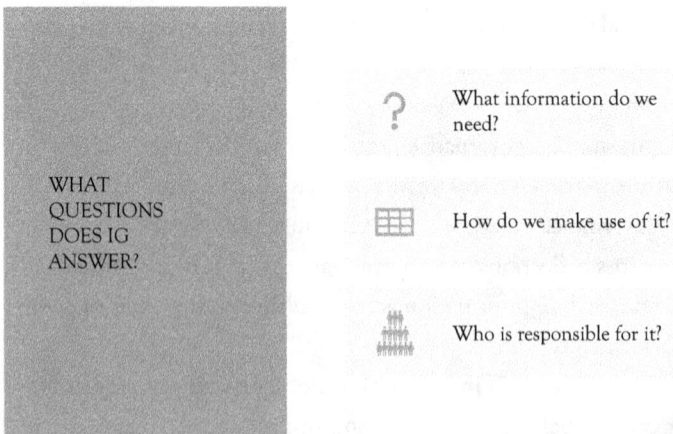

WHAT QUESTIONS DOES IG ANSWER?

?   What information do we need?

   How do we make use of it?

   Who is responsible for it?

Source: M.N. Kooper, R. Maes, and E.R. Lindgreen. 2011. On the governance of information: introducing a new concept of governance to support the management of information. *Int. J. Inf. Manage.* 31(3), 195–200.

Like these examples (of poor information governance practices), signs of strong information governance tend to center around the basic themes of cost reduction, improved regulatory response, better security, and improved employee engagement.

CHAPTER 5

Obstacles to Information Governance Improvement

What Is Standing in the Way of IG Success?

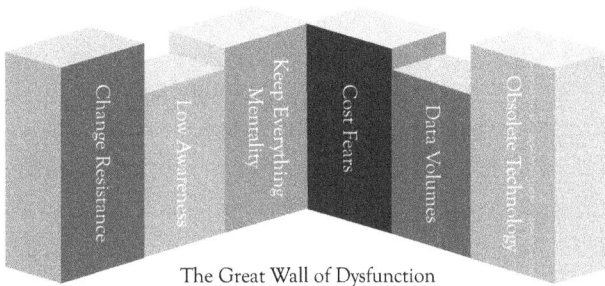

The Great Wall of Dysfunction

As with many complex organizations, research libraries can face significant challenges when seeking to improve or maintain their information governance practices. These challenges include:

- *Change resistance*: Improving information governance practices often requires organizations to make significant changes in the way they operate, which can be challenging for staff. Combatting this resistance requires a concerted effort to achieve buy-in by training staff and emphasizing the positive impact that information governance best practices can have on their work.
- *Lack of awareness*: Challenges can arise when employees do not see why they need to improve their practices. This is especially true for organizations like libraries that employ a mix of transient employees such as students and long-term workers.

- *Keep everything mentality*: Research libraries must comply with legal and regulatory requirements related to data management, privacy, and security. Also, many employees tend to see keeping everything as the surest way to comply with retention laws. This is not only dangerous in a legal sense (especially regarding privacy laws), but also costly and potentially risky, particularly in the case of litigation. Combatting this mentality requires research librarians to continually communicate the needs and importance of information governance best practices to their staff and to gauge staff buy-in on a regular basis.
- *Costs*: One of the main challenges that research libraries face is a lack of resources, including funding, staffing, and technology. Without adequate resources, it can be difficult to implement and maintain effective information governance practices. Therefore, it is critical for research libraries to secure the funding that they need for an information governance improvement project *before* the project begins and to maintain executive-level support within both the library and its parent organization throughout the engagement.
- *Data volumes*: Research libraries handle a huge volume of data in multiple formats, ranging from legacy formats such as microfilm to cloud storage and physical storage. Staff may not be "up-to-date" on the most current data management standards. This requires training, clear policies and procedures, and a concerted and unified approach to data management.
- *Obsolete systems/legacy technology*: Many research libraries use legacy systems that may not be compatible with modern information governance practices. Updating these systems can be costly and time-consuming, which can impede information governance progress. This issue is closely related to both "cost" and "awareness." Research libraries seeking to implement information governance practices must factor in the cost of upgrading systems and choosing the right repositories and storage formats.

CHAPTER 6

What Is the Role of a Modern Digital Librarian?

In today's world, librarians, and in particular, digital librarians, are responsible for managing numerous information systems, processes, and staff. These responsibilities require the adoption of a multifaceted skill set that requires a deep understanding of the importance of data and the ability to manage that data.[1]

The data must be clearly identified, organized, and archived, and to be successful, a modern digital librarian must be able to, among other tasks, clearly communicate the need for:

- Organizing and uniformly categorizing data
- Centralizing the management of data across an organization, in both online and offline forms
- Deleting unnecessary or expired data in a way that complies with applicable law
- In certain cases, complying with Freedom of Information Act Requests and otherwise making sure that data is properly delivered to all relevant stakeholders
- Helping to mitigate risks by balancing the need for information sharing with the goal of protecting data security
- Promoting copyright protection and otherwise helping to protect intellectual property rights

Given the multifaceted nature of these roles, it has become increasingly important for modern digital librarians to understand information governance principles and to deploy them to ensure that they are properly deployed.

---

[1] www.infotoday.eu/Articles/Editorial/Featured-Articles/The-many-hats-of-the-digital-librarian-121520.aspx.

CHAPTER 7

Why Big Data Is Such a Big Problem for Research Librarians?

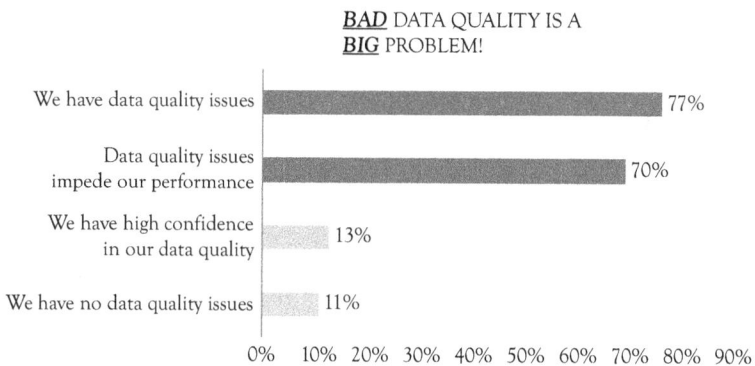

BAD DATA QUALITY IS A
BIG PROBLEM!

We have data quality issues	77%
Data quality issues impede our performance	70%
We have high confidence in our data quality	13%
We have no data quality issues	11%

0%   10% 20% 30% 40% 50% 60% 70% 80% 90%

Source: Information is based on a survey of 500 data professionals conducted by Great Expectations.

Managing big data is critical for research libraries because it enables them to make informed decisions and provide better services to their patrons and other stakeholders.

Oracle defines the term big data as data sets that contain greater variety and that arrive in increased volumes and with additional velocity. To provide an idea of the size of this data proliferation, according to Statista sources, there are about 64.2 zettabytes of data created, captured, copied, and consumed in the entire digital universe, a number that is likely to triple by 2025.[1]

That said, big data is a term that has yet to be operationally defined. From an analysis of 1,437 articles that discuss big data, word clouds with

---

[1] www.ifla.org/news/why-big-data-matters-perspectives-from-the-libraries/.

four centralized themes were identified. The four emergent themes include information, technology, methods, and impact. Big data can be defined as "the Information asset characterized by such a High Volume, Velocity, and Variety to require specific Technology and Analytical Methods for its transformation into value." Basically, big data about us is the process of accumulating past and present information on individuals in various areas of our lives, in order to rationally predict future behaviors or needs.[2] Volume represents the large amount of data that must be managed, while velocity refers to the speed at which the data can be collected and stored. Variety describes the different file types and sources with which organizations must contend. Veracity examines the quality of data, including whether it is unique or outdated; and value refers to the usefulness of the data to the organization.

While there are many innovative analytics tools in the market, most of them struggle to scale, and our ability to make sense of the volume, variety, and velocity of data we collect cannot currently keep pace with our ability to collect it. Sampling, or the methodical selection of a smaller data set for analysis, is an effective way to address this challenge. Poor sampling methods can lead to inaccurate conclusions, so it is important to focus on the accuracy and utility of the sample size.

One source of the unprecedented growth of data could be attributed to business adaption in response to COVID-19. In one survey published in World Economic Forum (WEF)'s Future of Jobs Report 2020, employers, and particularly those with significant numbers of home workers, are accelerating the digitalization of work processes as well as automation of tasks, generating more data in return. Companies in various sectors surveyed in the report also indicated that big data analytics, artificial intelligence, Internet of Things, and connected devices are some of the technologies likely to be adopted by 2025.

In addition, for libraries undertaking information governance projects, data science has become an increasingly important discipline, relying on formal scientific and statistical methods to extract actionable information and strategic knowledge from vast amounts of data. Data science is focused on solving big data problems, classifying and taxonomizing large

[2] https://asistdl.onlinelibrary.wiley.com/doi/10.1002/bul2.2017.1720430406.

amounts of structured, semistructured, and unstructured data. Unstructured files, such as text and rich media, are the most common data types encountered in information governance and e-discovery.

As a result, it has become increasingly critical for libraries, and especially research libraries, to aggressively manage the proliferation of big data and to take proactive strategies to use that data to further their overall goals. These goals include (without limitation):

- *Improving their understanding of patron/stakeholder needs*: Research libraries collect and analyze large volumes of data on their patrons' usage patterns, preferences, and interests, and strategies are needed to allow them better understand their needs. Big data analytics can be harnessed to develop more comprehensive targeted services and programs, as well as personalized recommendations.
- *Preservation of collections*: Research libraries are responsible for ensuring their collections are properly maintained and preserved. Big data analytics should be used to assess the physical condition of their collections, identify at-risk materials, differentiate between good- and bad-quality copies of books, and identify which records are the "right versions." These efforts are critical to research libraries' central goals of preserving the integrity of their collections and promoting their sustainability.
- *Improved resource allocation*: Research libraries, like other institutions, must continually seek ways to maximize the value of their resources and avoid waste. By aggressively analyzing data on resource usage, librarians can identify trends and patterns that can inform decisions on resource allocation. This helps libraries to optimize their budget and resources, ensuring that they are providing the most relevant and useful services to their patrons and stakeholders—besides the success of their information governance programs and process improvement efforts!
- *Facilitating research*: Most modern research (both academic and industry) depends on researchers' success in deriving

conclusions from large data sets. Appropriately harnessing big data analytics supports these research efforts by providing researchers with access to large and reliable data sets and tools for analysis, which in turn enables those researchers to conduct more comprehensive and in-depth research, leading to new discoveries and insights.

Here are some tangible examples of how major research libraries have used big data analytic solutions to improve their data management and resource allocation efforts.

In one noted example, in a project presented at the IFLA (International Federation of Library Associations and Institutions) WLIC 2022 conference in Dublin, the U.S. Library of Congress demonstrated how they harnessed physical, chemical, and optical data insights to make informed decisions on whether to retain or withdraw items from their cultural heritage collections, ensuring the overall robustness of their collections. This project exemplified how an organization's ability to collect, store, and analyze data sets can significantly enhance its capacity to make objective decisions.[3]

To address knowledge gaps and perform an objective assessment of their collections, they employed a data analytics approach to identify materials that were at risk and differentiate between good- and bad-quality copies of books.

The study examined over 500 identical books, published between 1840 and 1940, from five large research libraries located in different parts of the United States. A data platform was established to store the sampling data collected by various instruments, such as tensile strength and acidity. These data were stored in a JSON document store called CouchDB, along with nonscientific data for each book.

To analyze the data, the team had a query tool to assess discrete data points in real time, as well as a compare tool that utilized an open-source International Image Interoperability Framework (IIIF) viewer to evaluate photo documentation between books up close.

---

[3] www.ifla.org/news/why-big-data-matters-perspectives-from-the-libraries/.

When assessing preservation factors, the team focused on the impact of the material, environment, and usage. The study revealed that the inherent properties of paper at the time of production were the most critical factor for predicting the book's condition.

In another example cited by the IFLA, the National Library Board (NLB) of Singapore created a program that allows libraries to adapt their systems to be big data compatible and leverage cloud technologies, thereby allowing them to shift their focus to high-value tasks such as model training and designing user experience.

As part of this project, in 2019, the NLB utilized Amazon Personalize, a cloud-based machine learning recommendation service, which they deployed in the NLB to develop its new recommender service for personalized book and e-book recommendations. The service was deployed on NLB's website and mobile app.

By deploying a fully managed cloud service, the NLB avoided infrastructure and machine learning pipeline maintenance, benefitted from product enhancements and new algorithms without additional investments, and reduced upfront capital expenditures.

In addition, the team utilized an existing data warehouse containing transactional data to create a unified view of patrons, enabling them to understand borrowing patterns. They then focused on training the model to improve recommendations, such as reducing duplicate title recommendations of different formats and providing subject-based recommendations.

Finally, the NLB enhanced the user experience of the book recommendation feature offered on its digital touchpoints by developing its web service layer to incorporate additional parameters for improved personalization. In one example, they passed a patron's age from the digital touchpoint onto the recommender service to retrieve age-appropriate recommendations.[4]

---

[4] Id.

CHAPTER 8

The Role of Records and Information Management

Information and records management is crucial for research libraries as it ensures that information needed is secure and available to meet organizational obligations, while delivering services in a consistent and equitable manner and providing continuity in the event of a disaster. A good records management program must protect records from unauthorized access and meet statutory and regulatory requirements for archiving, audit, and oversight activities. This program should also provide protection and support during litigation, enable quick storage and retrieval of documents and information, and improve efficiency and productivity from an operational perspective.

Research libraries may be subject to a range of legal and regulatory requirements related to records and information management, including data privacy laws, copyright regulations, and freedom of information requests. A records management program can help ensure that the library is in compliance with these requirements and is able to respond to legal or regulatory requests in a timely manner.

The technology used to store and access information is critical for research libraries. Failure to maintain proper records and document management platform can result in a direct threat to the security, integrity, and availability of data, which could lead to any number of problems, including questions of veracity or authenticity due to a degradation of data quality. Compliance with legal and regulatory requirements for records management is essential for research libraries to safeguard data and information assets.

There are three phases for responsible records retention compliance: identification and retention, preservation and safekeeping, and destruction and disposal of records that have fulfilled their life cycle and outlived their usefulness. An up-to-date, comprehensive records and information management program documents the research library's intent and commitment to compliance, thus reducing potential punitive and compensatory damages that can result from litigation or regulatory fines.

Maintaining updated policies and procedures for the systematic control of records is exceptionally important for research libraries. Without proper records management, research libraries may be storing records too long, not long enough, or not at all. Worse, they may be prematurely destroying or spoliating vital documents. Failure to maintain records and data necessary for regulatory auditing, compliance reporting, and other valid organizational requirements presents a great risk, which can be mostly unreasonable, if not negligent, in this day and age.

Any risks related to noncompliance with records retention regulations could lead to penalties, blemished public reputation, and any number and variety of legal liabilities. RIM controls are needed to demonstrate proactive and transparent efforts to satisfy compliance requirements. Consistent records management processes, policies, and practices can also dramatically reduce litigation costs, in terms of both improved efficiency and mitigating or eliminating risk.

Ultimately, a proper records management function in research libraries ensures that records of vital historical, fiscal, and legal values are identified and preserved, while nonessential records are discarded in a timely manner according to established rules or guidelines.

With the increasing digitization of library collections, research libraries need to have robust records and information management practices in place to ensure that digital materials are properly preserved and accessible over time. This includes adherence to metadata standards, appropriate version control, and regular backups to guard against data loss.

Several use cases involving libraries are described below.

Research libraries often house valuable and unique archival collections, such as letters, manuscripts, photographs, and other documents. A records management program can help ensure that these materials are properly preserved and maintained for future generations, including through appropriate metadata and indexing.

Many research libraries receive funding from government agencies or other organizations that have specific requirements around records and information management. A records management program can help ensure that these requirements are met, including through proper retention and disposal of records.

Research libraries may also need to manage records related to their own institutional activities, such as financial records, personnel files, and meeting minutes. A records management program can help ensure that these records are properly maintained and disposed of according to legal and regulatory requirements.

CHAPTER 9

The Records Life Cycle

In the context of libraries, the records management life cycle refers to the process of managing the creation, use, retention, and disposal of records. The life cycle includes seven phases: creation and capture, collaboration and use, taxonomy and classification, version control and management, retention and archiving, preservation and hold, and disposition and destruction.

To effectively manage records, it is essential to identify, organize, and classify them using a taxonomy and retention schedule. This enables libraries to comply with laws and regulations governing the retention and disposal of records. Secure storage is also necessary to protect the records and ensure they remain accessible and reliable until they are no longer needed.

Before we return to the life cycle phases, first is a brief introduction to metadata, which is basically data about data and essential to the entire aforementioned data life cycle. It is the reason a document can be indexed, searched, enhanced, and grouped with or separated from other similar documents. It describes the document, who created or modified it, and when they created or modified it. An e-mail includes server information, senders and recipients, and whether it has attachments. It describes where it came from and where it resides and includes unique technical information, which ensure its uniqueness. It is used to determine access rights and whether it is related to other documents or clusters of documents. It can be hashed to create a unique fingerprint to identify it or eliminate duplicative copies. And over time, it will be enhanced to include everything that can be known about its journey during that life cycle, most importantly, when it was created, which retention rules or legal holds it may be subject to, and whether or when it can be destroyed.

Creation and capture represent the date, time, and file type the moment a document comes into existence. Once it exists, it can be used by one or many individuals who have the right to access it. If a number of individuals collaborate on a document it will be subject to version control, which will track and preserve changes among multiple users. Depending on the status of our users, whether they be on a legal hold or subject to regulatory retention, the document will be retained and archived with a set of rules to prevent it from being destroyed or spoliated. And finally, if the document should outlive its retention requirements, legal holds, and usefulness, it will be subject to destruction.

So, records need to be identified, organized, and classified using a taxonomy and retention schedule so that they can be managed, retained, retrieved, and disposed of in accordance with the laws and regulations which govern them. They must be securely stored to ensure that they are protected, accessible, and reliable until they are no longer of value to the organization or required due to regulations or legal holds. They should be inventoried in tandem with asset management and data mapping to ensure their accessibility and efficient access. Some modern tools enable and empower this process with automation. Their data quality and metadata should be preserved and enhanced over time to increase their value to the organization. They should be migrated and consolidated when it makes sense to improve security, availability, and searchability or to reduce duplicative costs. And again, a proactive destruction or disposition program reduces the risk of overretention, unnecessary storage costs, and improved bandwidth.

Data quality and records inventories are essential to quality records management and should be revisited by operations and compliance on a periodic basis. A completed record inventory can also provide each organization unit with information to enable better management and organizational intelligence. There are six important concepts to keep in mind when creating the records inventory: identifying required records to add to the inventory is likely to highlight duplicates and unnecessary retention of information. Adding records to the inventory will instigate discussions about whether efficiencies can be made in the volumes of information held and replicated. A data map will also be useful. Classification of records sets out clearly why records are held, what value they provide, and how they fit into the wider context of the organization.

Over time, the retrieval of records is improved when there is an accurate inventory of where they are stored. Use of records over time may change, including ownership and storage location. The inventory will help track those changes making long-term management of records easier. Understanding whether there is an ongoing requirement to retain records will in part be supported by the record inventory and the record classes that have been identified, which will help hedge against resignation in the form of the "keep everything" approach.

Finally, confidence in disposing of records starts with a clear link between records and retention schedules. The record inventory will make that link with structured and consistent governance. It will make for more effective management of data. It will help reduce and eliminate redundancies. It will reduce costs for storage and duplicative systems. It will reduce legal liability and monetary risk by avoiding spoliation. It can even hedge against cybersecurity breaches since you cannot hack what does not exist.

Use cases[1] illustrating the aforementioned records management life cycle principles in the context of library management can include the following:

Libraries often collect and preserve historical materials such as manuscripts, photographs, and audio recordings. The records management life cycle can help ensure these materials are stored securely, protected from damage or loss, and made accessible to researchers and other users.

Libraries are subject to various regulations governing the retention and disposal of records, such as data privacy laws or Freedom of Information Act requirements. The records management life cycle can help libraries comply with these regulations by ensuring records are properly classified, retained for the required length of time, and disposed of when no longer needed.

Libraries may collaborate with other organizations or individuals on projects that involve creating and sharing documents. The records management life cycle can help manage the creation and version control of these documents to ensure they are properly tracked, preserved, and accessible to all parties involved.

---

[1] Author's note: Many of the use cases and hypothetical fact patterns in this book were created with the aid of ChatGPT and similar AI programs and were based on detailed fact-specific queries.

CHAPTER 10

Data Governance

Data governance is a critical process for libraries as they manage large volumes of information. It involves managing, archiving, accessing, and controlling the exponential growth of data and data types that are now extending to thousands of platforms and applications. Libraries need to meticulously plan their data management from scope and architecture to policies, asset management, and operational frameworks, which serve organizational needs while meeting regulatory and compliance standards.

One significant challenge faced by libraries in managing data is the proliferation of redundant, obsolete, or trivial (ROT) data. The existence of this type of data is often the result of backups, multiple users, and inefficient data management, leading to dozens of copies of the same documents. The problem of ROT data can be mitigated by using deduplication, classification methods, and single-instance storage, which preserves a single version of a record with a reference pointer to the e-mails, documents, or file systems from where the file(s) originated.

An essential component of good data governance in libraries is asset management and data mapping. This involves protecting and backing up physical assets, including legacy systems, storage devices, and applications that present substantial risk and should be replaced and migrated from, as a part of the process of data life cycle management. Migrations provide an opportunity to port only those records that are still subject to retention requirements while leaving behind and destroying those which have outlived their retention schedules or usefulness.

Data consolidation into a single or federated archive is an effective way for libraries to reduce risks associated with compliance and security, reduce the potential for spoliation or unintended destruction, allow for more efficient retention and disposition, eliminate duplicative resources and risks, and reduce the inefficiency in maintaining an array of systems and subject matter experts. Consolidation also reduces the likelihood of data remediations and facilitates a more defensible, efficient, and reliable process overall.

A well-managed data governance program in libraries allows custodians and responsive data to be searched and extracted in hours and days. In organizations with poorly designed, integrated, and managed systems, the same process can often drag on for weeks and months, frustrating stakeholders, particularly in legal or compliance. Failure to identify, search, or extract data can be a major frustration to stakeholders who must review data or evidence and pass it on to regulators, investigators, or opposing counsel. Therefore, libraries must consider these risks and challenges when building a reliable and defensible enterprise data governance program.

Given are a few use cases illustrating good versus bad data governance practices for libraries:

Good Data Governance Practices

- A library invests in a modern library management system to manage their collection, users, and circulation processes. They also conduct regular reviews of their data to ensure they are not storing redundant, obsolete, or trivial data. They establish retention schedules and dispose of data that is no longer needed. They make sure their system is backed up and have a plan in place for data recovery in the event of system failure.

- A library consolidates their data into a single archive, which reduces the risk of data loss or duplication and makes it easier to maintain and manage their data. They have a clear plan for integrating different types of data and ensure that their archive is accessible, secure, and searchable.

- A library implements security protocols to safeguard sensitive data, such as patron information and circulation records. They limit access to this data to authorized staff and require secure authentication for access. They also have a process in place for detecting and responding to security incidents and have a disaster recovery plan in case of a security breach or other disaster. These security protocols should accord with ISO standards such as ISO 18128:2014, which provides a framework for federated authentication, a mechanism that allows users to access multiple systems or applications (such as the archives of multiple libraries operating within a system) using a single set of credentials.[1]

Bad Data Governance Practices

- A library fails to establish a retention policy for their data, which leads to data overload and increases the risk of data loss, duplication, and other issues. They continue to store data that is no longer needed, such as outdated circulation records, and fail to dispose of it in a timely manner.
- A library fails to maintain their library management system, which leads to outdated, unstable systems that are prone to failure. They also fail to back up their data, which increases the risk of data loss in case of system failure or other disaster.
- A library fails to implement appropriate security protocols for their data, such as failing to limit access to sensitive data or using weak authentication methods. They also fail to have a plan in place for detecting and responding to security incidents, which increases the risk of data breaches and other security incidents.

---

[1] ISO 18128:2014 includes topics such as the types of authentication protocols and technologies that should be used in a federated environment, the roles and responsibilities of the different entities involved in the authentication process, and the required security and privacy considerations.

CHAPTER 11

Records Management Surveys

The record survey is the primary source of information necessary to develop classification schemes, to associate retention schedules, and to understand one's organization. These surveys will also capture the information needed for our gap analysis, risk assessment, and vital records documents. These surveys consist of interviewing appropriate staff.

Essential elements of our approach are as follows:

- *Data collection*: It includes record types, activity patterns, and other related information.
- *Surveys and file evaluations*: The scope of the survey process will include interviews with users from departments that are significant generators of the aforementioned captioned records (in a scheduled series of meetings). During these meetings, any of our questions relevant to our projects should be answered.
- *Validation*: Review of survey data by one's staff will ensure validation by the data source.

For libraries, the record survey process can be adapted to gather information about the library's collection and how it is managed.

Use case: records management surveys for a university library—A university library conducts a record survey to gather information about its collection and how it is managed. The survey process involves interviewing staff from various departments, including circulation, acquisitions, and reference services, to ensure that all areas of the library are represented. The survey data is then used to develop a classification scheme and retention schedule for the library's collection, which is regularly reviewed and updated. The survey data is also used to identify any gaps in the collection, assess risks related to the collection, and identify any vital records. The survey data is validated by reviewing it with library staff to ensure accuracy and completeness. As a result of the regular record surveys, the university library has a well-managed collection that is organized, easily accessible, and adequately protected.

CHAPTER 12

Legal Research

The objective of this process is to identify the specific legal retention requirements, legal citations, and governing authorities for each record class.

The legal research project involves these subtasks:

- *Legal group classification*: Linking record classes to legal groups of records that are viewed similarly by the law or regulatory bodies.
- *Legal research*: A database of legal and compliance research is reviewed and updated to relate the law to the legal group and hence the record classes.
- *Auditing*: Interpreting and auditing the legal research.

Common records retention schedules display department, record class code, title descriptor, onsite retention, offsite retention, and other deemed headings from one's specific internal firm's needs.

Use case: A library has multiple types of records such as circulation records, interlibrary loan records, and patron records. The legal team needs to identify the specific legal retention requirements, legal citations, and governing authorities for each record class to ensure compliance with the law. They conduct legal research and audit the research to make sure that the records are being retained for the appropriate length of time. They then update the common records retention schedule with the relevant information to ensure that the library is following the law and retaining records appropriately.

CHAPTER 13

Governance and Steering Committees

A governance or steering committee is a group of executives or senior managers who provide guidance, authority, and approval on strategic initiatives in libraries and other organizations. This oversight mechanism is intended to ensure that the goals and objectives of key initiatives are aligned with organizational goals in general. As such, the steering committee will have the final authority on budgets, scope, and resources and meet periodically to ensure initiatives are headed in the proper direction. They will also help identify risks, prioritize key deliverables, and establish appropriate and measurable success criteria. A steering committee is generally led by a chairperson who is formally or informally elected and serves as a sort of mediator to keep the committee on track and help resolve disputes or disagreements. This is particularly important in complex organizations such as libraries, where different groups, teams, or entities are not just cross-impacted but have the potential to operate at cross purposes.

Considering the level of complexity in technology operations in libraries, a governance committee must also be able to rely on a team of senior subject matter experts who have the hands-on, day-to-day experience to advice on and support their strategic decisions. In most cases, they should have an intimate working knowledge of the subject areas at hand, including testing, validation, and key performance indicators. A common scenario, therefore, is a sort of triumvirate of executives, senior subject matter experts, and project management staff.

In most cases, a project manager will sit at the helm of each enterprise initiative in libraries to manage day-to-day activities, ensure deliverables are met on time, and serve as a focal point among various stakeholders. A project manager's job comes down to providing timely and accurate reporting or, in certain regards, serving as a single source of truth for the real-time status of the initiative. This will be true from the early stages of research and planning through execution and closure.

A project manager needs to have not just strong communication skills but a strong will, particularly in moments where they must inform a room full of executives something they might not necessarily want to hear. That being the case, a skilled project manager frames the challenges, risks, and workarounds in a succinct and informed manner that will allow the governance committee to make the most effective and educated decisions or course corrections. With good communication comes trust and confidence, and that usually starts with the truth.

Experienced leaders generally understand that projects rarely run according to plan. So, the expectation is not perfection, but that material issues will be escalated in a timely fashion. This will put them in the best position to do their jobs and provide guidance and leadership that will help get a project back on track and completed on budget and on time. Waiting too long on getting information to the governance committee for fear of a bad reaction can become a self-fulfilling prophecy. Not only does delayed information weaken their ability to make good decisions, but it also tends to reflect poorly on their leadership. In cases where critical information may be pending, unavailable, or incomplete, it is all the more vital to advise the governance committee what is known, any limitations of the current information, and that updates will be provided immediately as they become available. It is also recommended to formalize these escalation protocols to eliminate any gray areas.

There is no standard size of a governance committee in libraries and other organizations. It depends on the size of the initiative and the number of groups or organizations that may be directly or indirectly cross-impacted. Too few members tend to err on the side of underrepresentation. Too many members, alternatively, present the challenge of mob rule. In most cases, the governance committee may be composed of roughly five to eight members. There is a balance to be struck between representation and effectiveness, not to mention how difficult it is to get their attention to schedule regular meetings. In the best of all worlds, a project manager will effectively manage deliverables and keep the team properly informed so that the time, however limited, is time well spent.

Following are two use cases indicating good versus bad practices.

Good Practice

The governance committee of a library meets periodically to review and approve strategic initiatives, such as the implementation of a new library management system. The committee is composed of experienced leaders from various departments within the library, as well as subject matter experts in technology and project management. A project manager is designated to manage day-to-day activities and provide regular updates to the committee. The committee trusts the project manager to escalate any issues in a timely manner and provide updates on a regular basis. The project manager communicates effectively with the committee, presenting challenges and risks in a clear and concise manner, allowing the committee to make informed decisions. The committee is not overly large, consisting of about five to eight members, ensuring effective representation without succumbing to the challenges of mob rule.

Bad Practice

The governance committee of a library is composed of only a few members, who are not experienced leaders in the library or subject matter experts in the initiatives being discussed. The committee does not meet regularly, and when they do meet, they do not have a clear understanding of the initiatives being discussed. The project manager is not designated, leading to confusion and inefficiency in managing day-to-day activities. The project manager does not communicate effectively with the committee, withholding critical information for fear of a bad reaction. When issues do arise, they are not escalated in a timely manner, leading to delays and cost overruns. The committee is too small to provide effective representation, leading to underrepresentation and lack of diversity in decision making.

CHAPTER 14

Strategic Alignment

The goal of strategic alignment in the context of library management is to connect the library's strategic organizational needs with the structure, teams, and resources necessary within the library itself or its parent organization, to operate as efficiently as possible. Just like any functioning system, any flaw within the library's structure or that of its parent entity can compromise its success. Libraries that fail to appreciate the importance of strategic alignment or do not know how to improve it can face significant risks.

Strategic alignment in libraries involves four principal areas: budget, technology, operations, and legal. Library management must drive the strategic goals and objectives and perform necessary research and analysis to plan initiatives, estimate return on investment (ROI), and collaborate with operations, technology, legal, and third parties to implement organizational plans. The library also needs to form the foundation of the leadership and governance committee, which will drive support and development.

Once the library has established a need for a project or initiative, the appropriate stakeholders will be brought to the table. The technical operations team will help determine the most effective plan to execute. They will work with budget and operations to determine scale and infrastructure, as well as the resources required to support a successful initiative. Operations will work closely with technology to provide project management and technical oversight, which includes reporting metrics and other means by which the governance committee can assess whether the project is on track and headed to successful completion. They will also begin by including factors that ensure security and organizational continuity. Finally, legal will adjudicate risk, defensibility, compliance, and any other matters that present legal risk or exposure to the library.

Following are several use cases illustrating the concept of strategic alignment in the library management context.

Developing a new digital service for library patrons: The library wants to offer a new digital service to its patrons, but it needs to ensure that it aligns with the library's strategic goals and objectives. The library will work with the appropriate stakeholders to determine the most effective plan to execute the project, including the technology infrastructure, budget, and legal considerations.

Implementing a new library management system: The library needs to implement a new library management system that aligns with its strategic goals and objectives. The library will work with the technical operations team to determine the most effective plan to execute the project, including the technology infrastructure, budget, and legal considerations. The library will also work closely with operations to ensure a smooth transition to the new system.

Reducing the library's carbon footprint: The library wants to reduce its carbon footprint, which aligns with its strategic goals and objectives. The library will work with the appropriate stakeholders to determine the most effective plan to execute the project, including the technology infrastructure, budget, and legal considerations. The library will also work closely with operations to ensure that the project aligns with its overall sustainability strategy.

CHAPTER 15

Strategic Vision

Strategic management vision is just as important in library management as it is in a competitive market. Without a clear vision, a library may lack direction, purpose, and cohesion. A strong vision statement can communicate where the library is heading in the long term and help guide decision making at all levels of management. In a highly competitive market, a library's vision can be the difference between success and failure.

However, developing a vision is not always easy. It requires research, analysis, and an understanding of the library's unique market and community. A library leader must have the capacity to imagine a better or more efficient way for the library to operate in the future and be able to inspire their team to work toward that common goal. This requires setting challenging but achievable targets that push the team beyond what they thought was possible, while also avoiding targets that are so difficult that they ensure failure.

Just like in a competitive market, a library's vision should lead to concrete goals and meticulous planning. A library's information governance goals should be the by-product of its vision, and the execution of those goals should confront obstacles and convert the vision into reality. Ultimately, a strong vision can be a unifying principle that gives the library a sense of common purpose and direction when it seeks to promote and implement information governance best practices. It should inspire individuals with the enthusiasm and energy to work together to achieve a common goal and provide a clear path for the library's future success.

A use case for this need is illustrated by the following scenario.

A library system wants to implement an information governance program to ensure the proper management of its electronic resources, including e-books and databases. The library's vision is to provide easy access to information and resources for its patrons while ensuring compliance with relevant laws and regulations.

To achieve this vision, the library creates an information governance committee consisting of representatives from different departments, including IT, legal, and operations. The committee develops policies and procedures for the acquisition, management, and retention of electronic resources, taking into account factors such as licensing agreements, copyright laws, and privacy regulations.

The committee also implements a metadata management system to ensure accurate and consistent metadata across all electronic resources, which improves discoverability and accessibility for patrons. The system includes guidelines for metadata creation, maintenance, and mapping to ensure that metadata adheres to industry standards and best practices.

To ensure ongoing compliance and effectiveness of the information governance program, the committee establishes regular reviews and audits of policies and procedures, as well as training and awareness programs for library staff on the importance of proper information management and governance.

Through this information governance program, the library is able to achieve its vision of providing easy access to information and resources for its patrons while also ensuring compliance with relevant laws and regulations. The program improves the management of electronic resources, enhances the discoverability and accessibility of information for patrons, and reduces the risk of legal and compliance issues.

CHAPTER 16

Organizational Drivers

Organizational drivers are the collective resources and activities that contribute to operational or financial outcomes. An organization relies on goals and objectives, which in turn require an intimate understanding of the resources that combine to achieve those—measurable and achievable—objectives. They include, but are by no means limited to, quality and quantity of human resources, organization locations, costs, production, social media presence, and so on. It is therefore critical to understand organizational drivers along with their strengths, limitations, and codependencies.

Of course, each organizational challenge is unique and requires a process of assessment and analysis to accurately identify key variables, which is recursive in nature. That is, to solve a problem, one must have a thorough understanding of its underlying root causes, as well as the chain of causes and effects that lead to it.

Organizational drivers are critical for the success of a library, which relies on goals and objectives to provide quality services and resources to its patrons. Understanding the resources and activities that contribute to operational or financial outcomes is essential for libraries to thrive. These drivers include, but are not limited to, the quality and quantity of staff, library locations, collection development, marketing, and community engagement.

It goes without saying that organizational drivers and metrics operate hand in hand. Specifically, variables must be quantified to make accurate representations up and down the food chain, especially for the purpose of building accurate financial assumptions and projections. And the amount of time and resources given to a problem is generally proportional to its overall impact.

One use case for organizational drivers in library management is the development of a new library branch. Understanding the community demographics, including population size, age, and educational back-ground, is a critical driver in determining the success of a new branch. This information helps the library leadership team to make informed decisions about the location, size, and services offered at the new branch. Additionally, understanding the library's budget and funding sources, as well as the availability of staff and resources, will impact the feasibility of opening a new branch.

Another use case for organizational drivers in library management is the implementation of a new technology or service. Understanding the library's current technology infrastructure, including hardware, software, and staff expertise, is critical in determining the feasibility and success of a new technology or service. Additionally, understanding the library's user base and their technology needs and preferences is essential in developing a service that meets their needs. This information can help library leadership to make informed decisions about the resources needed to implement the new technology or service.

CHAPTER 17

Strategic Planning

Strategic planning is an essential part of library management, enabling libraries to align their activities with their vision and goals. Strategic planning involves the development of a comprehensive plan that outlines specific and measurable actions, objectives, and resources necessary for execution. It is a process that requires a clear understanding of the library's key organizational drivers, including its strengths, limitations, and codependencies.

Strategic planning should be driven and supported by the executive leadership of the library or its parent institution, with the support of the library's project managers (PMs). The strategic vision of the library should then be translated into a series of finite goals, which are then reverse-engineered into a methodical structure in the form of constituent and dependent tasks. A comprehensive project plan is then developed with as much detailed information as possible, including objectives, resources, budgets, deliverables, and risk controls. PMs play a critical role in the success of strategic planning, working closely with leadership and staff to ensure the project plan is achievable and comprehensive.

Strategic planning should involve stretching limitations and being just a little uncomfortable, balancing options and budgets to facilitate a degree of certainty. An innovative library or library system should encourage strategic thinking and, if so, is more likely to endure conditions when they do not go precisely according to plan or when circumstances on the ground require a pivot in direction or tactics. A risk response strategy provides protection, and a PM with risk management experience can help to reduce risks, although no guarantee can be made that risks will be eliminated. Leadership provides guidance and strategic thinking to the project management team.

In the library context, the specifics of a project plan depend entirely on the nature of the library and the project. A plan to digitize a library's collection, for example, will require an extraordinarily rigorous and exacting plan, whereas a plan to launch a summer reading program may require specific details without excessive details. The specificity of a project plan is based on the organization's requirements and risks, appropriate to their needs and goals.

Following are several use cases illustrating the concept of strategic planning in the context of library management.

Strategic planning for a library digitization project: A library wants to digitize its entire collection to provide greater access to users. The library's executive leadership works with the project management team to develop a comprehensive project plan that includes objectives, resources, budgets, deliverables, and risk controls. The plan also includes a risk response strategy to mitigate the risks associated with such a large-scale project. The PM works closely with the library staff to ensure the project plan is achievable and comprehensive.

Strategic planning for a library marketing campaign: A library wants to increase its visibility in the community and attract more users. The library's executive leadership works with the project management team to develop a comprehensive project plan for a marketing campaign that includes objectives, resources, budgets, deliverables, and risk controls. The plan also includes a risk response strategy to mitigate the risks associated with the marketing campaign. The PM works closely with the library staff to ensure the project plan is achievable and comprehensive.

Management Principles

The sophistication and complexity of management theory is slowly catching up to the sophistication of our technological advancement in an increasingly complex global marketplace—and this is true, even for traditional institutions such as libraries. In some regards, it might seem the reverse would be true; that is, to design effective systems we must ourselves become more systematic and robotic, for lack of a better phrase. That is only half true. Indeed, we can and should increasingly rely on formal and semiformal systems to improve and maximize process efficiency while minimizing human error. But most of us are not robots and do not wish to be treated as such, which largely explains why the vast majority of turnover can be attributed to a sense that management often undervalues and underappreciates its employees. While we often talk about people, process, and technology, managers can often confuse people with process or technology and reduce them to components. A good manager is sensitive to human complexity while recognizing the systematic nature of process and organization to maximize human potential. Fortunately, as it turns out, what is best for employees is often what is best for management and the organization at large. The current market for knowledge workers is also having a restorative effect. With greater mobility and opportunity than ever, skilled employees, particularly in technology, need not be reduced to automatons.

At the same time, and somewhat paradoxically, organizations are becoming more process and data oriented, which provides the objectivity necessary to remove or at least minimize emotion and personality from the task at hand. But any good and effective manager has to understand, first and foremost, that they are working with human beings, who have friends and families, hopes and dreams, and personal and professional aspirations. Which is why a manager should spend time looking inward and considering how he or she is perceived by employees and whether the fealty they command is through respect or fear. Are their employees excited to go to work? Do they like, or at least, respect their boss or the people with whom they share the majority of their waking hours? And how, if at all, are those perceptions impacting productivity?

It seems obvious that a manager should want to earn the respect of his employees. But too often they are more interested and invested in their own success, even at the expense of their team. Satisfied employees and doing good hard work are not mutually exclusive—a type of obsolescent thinking that goes back to the early industrial revolution. But let us be clear: while soft skills are crucially important to good leadership and good management, they are by no means a replacement for experience or expertise. A poor leader or manager can make a successful career for themselves being a creep who happens to be very skilled at their job. Whether they have any meaningful or trusting relationships is another story.

A manager should also make an effort to establish trust with employees. It is especially effective to reinforce the notion that their privacy and confidentiality will be respected. This in turn encourages greater trust and honesty between the boss and subordinate, which is better for the team and the individual. Employees often become discouraged when their superiors appear not to value their ideas or recommendations or at least give them the light of day. For selfish and unselfish purposes, it can be useful to let them know that, even if their ideas or suggestions fail to make it past the concept stage, they will nevertheless get a hearing. By the same token, a manager should give credit where credit is due. One who takes credit for others' efforts will never be respected or establish trust. Alternatively, there are times when mistakes must be revealed or papered over. A manager who turns mountains into mole hills merely to exert power will similarly fail to earn the esteem of his employees. People make mistakes. Unless it is the end of the world, a good manager should use leadership jujitsu to convert a mistake or error of judgment into a constructive learning experience, which will also increase the probability of greater respect and trust with one's employees in the future.

Another underrepresented skill among managers is the ability to recognize aptitude and, to the extent possible, orient employees in a direction that will have the most productive impact on the team, on the organization, and on their careers. Different people have different personalities, interests, and aptitudes. A manager should take the time to learn where an employee's sweet spots are to increase the probability of their success, as well as the overall capacity of the team. It may be wise, for example, not to force one's introverted database manager into the role of client success manager. Or select an employee who is uncomfortable speaking in pubic to conduct critical presentations. There is always an opportunity to discuss such matters with employees, if only we would find the time. Even if the exercise in no way changes the substance of their job or the direction of their career, they will recognize and appreciate the effort, and both will learn something in the process.

Indeed, there are times when a manager has little choice but to do the best with the team he or she has. So, if certain exigencies require that creative or talented employees pull staples on a particular day, then so be it. A wise manager will acknowledge when a job is unpleasant or distasteful and make light of it rather than displaying a lack of sympathy—or worse, gaslight employees by pretending it is not that bad. It also would not kill a manager to use it as an opportunity for team building or find painless ways to make it up to them.

To be clear, none of this is to suggest employees be coddled; or are not obliged to maintain ownership and accountability; or are not responsible for their mistakes and missteps; or can in any way take their time management or their deliverables for granted; or do not have a professional obligation to their manager and their team; or that they need not follow rules or process requirements. Nothing about being a good manager suggests a diminution of employee responsibilities. In fact, it is the opposite one should expect in a give-and-take relationship.

Though it does not always come naturally, a manager must learn to be flexible and adaptive to change, especially in an increasingly dynamic and complex global environment. A manager who can pivot with the technology and the times will stand out to executive management. Excessive rigidity on the other hand often leads to poor adaption, poor communication, and poor outcomes. It is at times necessary to teach and, more often, to learn, and the best managers tend to be the best students, whether they acquire skills formally or informally. But good and poor habits are all a matter of practice. Invest in good skills and good communication and you will generally receive dividends over time.

A struggle that often arises and can pit a manager between his employees and executive leadership is training. Most employees see the value for themselves and for the organization in improving their skills, especially when those efforts are acknowledged and reciprocated. Regrettably, many enterprises undervalue the virtue of training and developing their employees. Thus, when putting budgets together, education and employee training often get short shrift. By contrast, more innovative organizations tend to invest more time and effort training their employees, realizing not just the benefits of improved efficiency and performance, but employee satisfaction. Conversely, enterprises who do not invest in their employees tend to receive negative returns on their investment in the form of low employee satisfaction.

Considering the type of effective, low-cost training available today, there are not a lot of good reasons for more focus on training. Surveys repeatedly indicate that, while salary is of course especially important, employees tend to be more motivated by job fulfillment. If an employee believes his boss and his firm are loyal and have his or her best interests at heart, they are much less likely to jump ship. But even if it were the case that better trained employees were leaving in modest numbers—and it is not obvious—it would nevertheless be to the firm's advantage to have better skilled employees during their employment. Whether one is a manager or employee, improvement requires time, investment, and commitment.

It is critically important for a manager to have a strong relationship with his or her PMs. Where the ultimate accountability rolls up to a manager, having weak PMs is a ticking time bomb. A manager also needs to be effective and maximize human potential. So, delegation is also important, as is becoming solutions oriented and improvement minded, that is, proactive in terms of always looking for a better solution or greater efficiencies and encouraging the team, as a team, to do the same.

At the end of the day, managers and employees must have accountability. So, like much in life, there needs to be a balance—for example, expressing empathy and trust on the one hand, and strength on the other. Sure, employees want a sympathetic leader but not at the expense of one who is competent and worthy of respect.

Understanding one's strengths and weaknesses is crucial to good leadership, as well as surrounding oneself with a talented team of individuals. Some managers of a lower order of primate can become jealous or politically concerned if they have employees who they believe might outshine them. This betrays a transparently flawed character. The best managers will look smart by surrounding themselves with talent so that the whole of their collective efforts is always greater than the sum of its parts.

Last of all, managers and employees alike should have a realistic understanding of their limitations or opportunities. Many of us focus on our strengths rather than our weaknesses and then wonder why our careers are in limbo. Or receive a less than stellar review and, instead of taking personal responsibility, let our egos blame our managers or co-workers. It is similarly ironic how often individuals fail to apply best organizational practices to their own lives or profession. One should conduct a periodic needs assessment and review of the objective data available to visualize a better, more fulfilling future state. We should all want to be the best version of ourselves in whatever we do. But organizational or personal change requires more than motivational speeches and self-help books; it requires a plan and executing that plan. Having a mentor in or out of the workplace is also advisable.

Project Management

In the context of libraries undertaking information governance projects, project management is a crucial methodology that enables planning, executing, and monitoring projects to completion within a specific timeframe. Information governance projects, such as those related to data management or compliance, require careful planning and execution to achieve their goals successfully.

In this context, ongoing work related to customer or technical services can be managed and errors or issues that require resolution can become distinct projects. The project life cycle for information governance projects in libraries consists of initiation, planning, execution, and closure.

During project initiation, the high-level goals, scope, risks, and dependencies of the information governance project should be established, and roles and responsibilities should be assigned. In the planning phase, details of resources, costs, deliverables, and timelines should be refined, and a single-page project charter should be created to communicate the project's core elements. Communication and reporting are crucial for the success of the project, and the PM should be responsible for collecting, recording, centralizing, and sharing information and metrics with stakeholders.

The project charter should summarize the key information about the project, including senior management, key players, goals, scope, success criteria, risks, dependencies, and what is out of scope. Time in project management for information governance projects in libraries refers to the aggregate number of hours required for a task, and duration is the overall timeframe in which the task will be completed.

In the context of libraries undertaking information governance implementation projects, time management is crucial for the successful completion of the project. The implementation of information governance requires careful planning, execution, and monitoring of the project to ensure that it is completed within a specific timeframe.

The PM must estimate the aggregate number of hours required for each task and the overall timeframe in days, weeks, months, and so on, in which the task will be completed. This will involve communicating with team members to assess how long it will take for them to complete their activities and whether it will impact the overall project timeline. The PM must also go beyond the surface to get a thorough understanding of the work requirements, resource availability, and reliability, especially for resources attached to critical path tasks.

A good project plan will have alternative or tactical solutions ready as necessary, connected to a PM's risk response assessment. For example, there is a backup plan if a key resource quits or there is a competing exigency that commands their time or attention.

Communication with resources on a regular, and often daily, basis is crucial, as is estimating time, which has a direct impact on budgets and completion dates. Making decisions about work and time based on guesswork can be calamitous. It is not unusual to make educated guesses during the process, but they are not so much guesses as well-researched and well-considered due diligence.

The nature or complexity of the project will dictate how long it will take to complete. For example, a data migration or disposition project could take months or even years, depending on the amount of data to be analyzed, searched, copied, or classified.

In addition, a wise PM should not rely solely on their team's representations. Precise estimation of work takes effort, time, and understanding all variables and unknowns that can impact it. Therefore, it is advisable for PMs to take a relatively conservative approach to estimating deliverables to avoid a negative cascade that reflects poorly on the PM and the team in general. PMs must also understand that a lack of dependability from a resource may not be due to a subpar performance but because they are higher performing and overtasked. In such cases, a PM should communicate with program management to ascertain whether competing work or projects might impact the resource's availability.

Having a program or portfolio management office can help ensure consistent standards for documentation, tools, processes, and reporting.

A good project management system should simplify complex tasks and take up as little time, energy, and communication as possible. Kanban boards or similar project management tools, for example, are becoming increasingly popular due to their simplicity, efficiency, and malleability.

During the project execution phase, the more time and consideration dedicated to planning and risk mitigation, the smoother and more efficient the execution stage will be. Human beings are flawed, including managers, and can make mistakes that can be costly. However, having a culture that values honesty, communication, trustworthiness, and teamwork can help mitigate these mistakes. PMs must also avoid thinking too high level and must have hands-on knowledge and understanding of the project to ensure its success.

Similarly, one of the more common blunders is thinking too high level when more hands-on knowledge or understanding is necessary or critical, or making assumptions about a challenge, process, or deliverable which may appear minor, but which could theoretically sabotage or at least threaten the success of the entire project. If for no other reason than protecting one's caboose, it is wise to perform the proper due diligence and not leave anything to chance.

The term RACI in project management means that roles should be established based on who is responsible, accountable, consulted, and informed. There are several variations on this theme, but they all essentially address the same challenge of clarifying roles and responsibilities. It may seem obvious to the uninitiated, but it is an area too often ignored or underestimated, particularly in less formal project management settings. It might be less critical on smaller projects with fewer personalities, responsibilities, and moving parts, but it is still highly recommended. A project with merely two or three stakeholders can go sideways, so there is frankly no good reason for trying to avoid confusion. Documenting roles and responsibilities is useful not just for communicating duties or obligations to various stakeholders, but as part of the project documentation overall. It is often the case that a historical project may inform a similar implementation in the future.

Similarly, after our planning and hard work, when we finally arrive at the end of the project, we must secure our planning materials and documentation to soberly reflect on our successes and failures. Did we meet or fail to meet our success criteria and to what extent? What did we miss during planning or execution? What could we have done better? Once a project is completed, everyone tends to move on very quickly and set their sights on the next priority. Where a project has not run particularly smoothly, that is the time people are less likely to want to revisit errors or misjudgments. But, of course, there is no better time or opportunity, which is the point of a lessons-learned exercise. Little surprise, then, when many of the mistakes or inefficiencies in an organization are repeated from project to project. A fresh review of a project at its conclusion, however brief, much less uncomfortable, will increase the probability of a more efficient project in the future. Needless to say, but if that exercise is not conducted constructively and with a certain degree of sensitivity, it could devolve into throwing one another under the bus, which defeats the purpose of the exercise in the first place. So, it is even more important for senior managers to take the lead while also assuming the role of crisis negotiator.

That said, it bears repeating that accountability is no less crucial to improvement, and a lack of accountability will not only encourage a repeat of poor performance but have a destructive effect on morale and cohesion for those who did perform well. Still, if a team member did not pull their weight, it is often better to have that conversation in private. Embarrassing one's employees helps no one and undermines morale and trust, as employees might have good reason to believe they could suffer the same embarrassment at a point in the future. Alternatively, there may be less obvious reasons to explain their inadequate performance such as overburdening them with work when they had limited bandwidth.

CHAPTER 18

Third-Party Vendor Management

In the context of information governance implementation projects by libraries or library systems, the need to manage and control relationships with vendors and suppliers is becoming increasingly demanding. The most obvious risks involve security breaches or organizational continuity failures. A good vendor management program should ensure that the relationships with vendors and suppliers provide maximum benefits while minimizing risks and help with cost containment measures.

A vendor manager should be responsible for supply chain management, contract negotiations, reporting, procurement, audit, and documentation. They must find a balance between holding the vendor's feet to the fire and working as partners and equals. It is critical to anticipate challenges, legal or otherwise, by scrupulously documenting all material interactions as if every line of a contract, every issues log, and every quarterly and annual organizational review could be used in a future litigation. The greater the discipline applied to the relationship, the greater the service in return.

A successful request for proposal (RFP) requires that all stakeholders participate throughout the entire process, with involvement proportional to the need and expertise. There is often so much at stake in terms of time and opportunity cost; therefore, the vendor manager must insist on full cooperation. A good prospective vendor will ask and understand most or all the pertinent questions about one's organizational needs. It is equally important to develop specifications and requirements that can be clearly and concisely communicated to vendors so both parties are on the same page in terms of expectations.

In the world of information governance vendor management for libraries, experienced IT or information governance professionals have learned from past mistakes. They have encountered vendors who have excelled in demos and RFPs but have failed to deliver in real-world conditions. Therefore, it is crucial to assess a platform or service's performance at scale and gather references and recommendations. A well-prepared list of questions and topics should be used to evaluate the vendor and service to determine how they are likely to perform. Inconsistencies between references should raise red flags or require maximum protection in the contract.

The process for vendor management usually begins with a perception of a need, which leads to brainstorming and information gathering. Demos with vendors follow, and the scope begins to narrow, leading to an RFP. All stakeholders should participate throughout the process, with involvement proportional to the need and expertise. The development of specifications and requirements should be clear and concise to communicate expectations. Depending on the scope, the process could be informal or take years.

A good vendor will ask pertinent questions to understand the organizational needs and translate the problem into detailed specifications. They will also assess whether their product or service is a suitable solution and determine whether the organization is seeking a new product or process or replacing an older one. If the latter, they will identify why the previous vendor failed and what the expectations are for the replacement. Sales and marketing will initiate these conversations, but technical SMEs will eventually take over to facilitate decisions and be responsible for implementation, maintenance, future performance, and vendor interaction.

Two significant red flags during the vendor selection process come down to politics and expertise. Every day, an objective effort to assess, grade, and select a vendor is undermined by political maneuvering. Years of effort can be undermined over a single cup of coffee between two executives. The combination of authority and a lack of applied knowledge and expertise are often destructive and demoralizing to a team who may have spent years carefully and diligently trying to make the right strategic decision for the organization only to have it upended by hubris and abuse of authority. While this is not something for which there is a surefire cure, a vendor manager and a team should document all their risks and concerns to the executive management team responsible for the final decision.

Finally, Service Level Agreements (SLAs) represent the specific services a vendor is providing and the level of service a client expects to receive to support them. To the extent possible, a vendor manager should try to negotiate the best SLAs that cover all features, functions, customizations, and audits or other hurdles for more favorable terms when, as is inevitably the case, the contract must be extended or renegotiated.

To build a mutually beneficial relationship, the vendor must deliver as promised, and the client must extract as much value as possible from the product, service, and relationship. Good, reliable vendor service is crucial, even beyond the value of technology, as the inability of a vendor to properly support technology may render it useless.

A smaller vendor with cutting-edge technology may possess transparency about its challenges in scaling and supporting it, and partnering with a larger firm may benefit both parties. The SLAs will describe the services, the vendor's scope of responsibility in delivering and managing those services, quality expectations, response time expectations, monitoring and reporting processes, and the expected start and end dates of the services.

Renewal or termination dates must also be included. Critical services will have steeper support fees and are the most difficult terms to negotiate. Instituting well-reasoned metrics and KPIs is also critical in monitoring and documenting performance, as well as more descriptive and qualitative metrics, including targets and baselines, which have become increasingly standard. Dashboards, scorecards, and automated reports are valuable tools for both the client and the vendor. Scorecards will represent performance in both qualitative and quantitative terms and weigh certain requirements based on criticality.

Given are several examples of good versus bad case scenarios in the context of vendor and third-party management for information governance implementation projects in libraries or library systems.

Good Case Scenario

A library system is looking to implement a new integrated library system (ILS) to replace their outdated system. The vendor management team follows a thorough process, starting with brainstorming and information gathering, followed by conversations and demos with vendors. They develop clear specifications and requirements and involve all stakeholders throughout the entire process. They also gather references and recommendations and conduct a proof-of-concept phase to ensure the system operates at scale in real-world conditions. They select a vendor who is responsive, is communicative, and has a track record of successful implementations. The vendor team works closely with the library system's information governance team to customize the system to meet their needs and provides excellent ongoing support. The library system experiences a smooth transition to the new ILS, with minimal disruptions to service and a high level of satisfaction from staff and patrons.

Bad Case Scenario

A library system is looking to implement a new discovery layer for their digital resources. The vendor management team rushes through the process, without thorough planning, specifications, or involvement from all stakeholders. They select a vendor based on a few glowing recommendations and a flashy demo, without conducting a proof-of-concept phase or reviewing references in detail. The vendor team promises customization and ongoing support, but is slow to respond to requests and doesn't have the expertise needed to address complex technical issues. The library system experiences significant disruptions to service, including downtime, incorrect search results, and poor user experience. The vendor team is unresponsive or defensive when issues are raised, and the library system is forced to invest significant time and resources in fixing problems and mitigating risks. Staff and patrons are frustrated and unhappy with the new system, and the library system's reputation is damaged.

CHAPTER 19

Continuous Improvement

Continuous improvement is a formal methodology that can benefit libraries that are seeking to undertake information governance projects by identifying and executing opportunities for improvement incrementally, minimizing disruption to operations and the organization. The approach emphasizes the reciprocal relationship between improving products, services, or processes and engaging employees to encourage constructive feedback and engagement.

Implementing major organizational transformations can often prove to be challenging for libraries and their staff. Change is an inevitable aspect of human nature, and employees can become habituated and comfortable with systems and processes, preferring the "devil they know," even if changes have the potential to make their jobs easier or processes more efficient. Additionally, cynicism can arise within the library if senior management makes top-down changes without input from the teams who perform the work or develop the very processes and systems. Changes sold as improvements can fail to live up to the benefits advertised, often because they were not properly vetted or tested in the first place.

Continuous improvement methodology is critical in engaging library employees as a value within the organizational culture, as they know best where the shoe pinches. Strong library managers and organizations understand that treating employees with trust and loyalty breeds trust and loyalty in return, as well as greater ownership and accountability. Encouraging constructive feedback on issues or inefficient processes generally comes at little or no cost, and it is hard to conceive of how less feedback and input from a team is better than more feedback.

Continuous improvement programs have made a resurgence in recent years, with different systems and verticals sharing the same basic objectives: to commit the library to a culture of improvement, demonstrate employee value, extract intelligence from staff, improve trust and communication, never settle for the status quo, and maintain a structure that can evolve to changing circumstances.

Intentionally or not, managers sometimes get lost in the stress and urgency of their job and forget that patrons include real human beings who depend on the library for their information needs. They have families and friends and hopes and dreams. They want to trust the library as a reliable source of information; to be treated respectfully and taken seriously and believe they are valued members of the community. Strong libraries understand that treating patrons with trust and loyalty breeds trust and loyalty in return, as well as greater ownership and accountability. Not to mention the fact that encouraging constructive feedback on issues or inefficient processes generally comes at little or no cost. Assuming it takes up very little of their time, it is hard to conceive of how less feedback and input from a team is better than more feedback.

According to the theory of "the wisdom of the crowd," the collective opinion of the group is statistically more effective or accurate than single or fewer individuals. Imagine a visualization where each point of a scatterplot represents an idea to be considered before making important strategic decisions. It is a scientific fact that the more—diverse and informed—opinions one considers, the higher probability of success that decision will tend to produce. This is not to suggest that library managers will or should make decisions based solely on statistical probability. It is simply to convey the idea that we should value our patrons, both because they are human beings and because they possess intrinsic value to a library merely by virtue of their potential to contribute good ideas.

In terms of risk and reward, our instincts to fear dramatic change are not entirely without merit. The greater the change, the greater the risk. Incremental change allows us to make significant improvements in real time while measuring the impact and minimizing risk. So, it provides us an opportunity to analyze whether our proposed changes have led to actual improvements or whether a pivot may be necessary to seek out a better solution. And a pivot from incremental change is naturally easier than a pivot from a more dramatic commitment.

Formal or semiformal continuous improvement programs have made a resurgence in recent years, manifesting in different systems and verticals, but all sharing the same basic objectives: to commit the library to a culture of improvement; demonstrate patrons have value; extract intelligence from staff; improve trust and communication; never settle for the status quo; and maintain a structure that can evolve to changing circumstances.

Six Sigma offers a simple blueprint for continuous improvement represented by the acronym DMAIC, which stands for define, measure, analyze, improve, and control. First, define, detail, and document an opportunity for change and improvement; second, establish the way in which data can be used to quantify and measure performance; third, analyze the variables from a data perspective to isolate and determine root causes; fourth, develop a solution that will remediate or improve those root causes; and fifth, execute, monitor, and maintain those solutions by establishing proper controls.

The following scenario highlights how Six Sigma processes can be successfully deployed in the context of implementing a library-based information governance implementation project:

- First, the library defines and documents the opportunity for change and improvement, such as improving the organization and accessibility of their digital assets.
- Next, they establish a way to measure and quantify performance, such as the average time it takes to locate and retrieve a digital asset or the number of errors encountered in the process.
- Then, using data from their measurements, the library can analyze the variables to identify the root causes of inefficiencies or errors in the digital asset management process. For example, they may discover that the search functionality in their digital asset management system is not working effectively, resulting in longer search times and lower efficiency.
- With this information, the library can develop and implement a solution that will remediate or improve the root cause. This might involve upgrading the digital asset management system or training staff on more effective search techniques.

- The library would then execute, monitor, and maintain the solution by establishing proper controls, such as tracking search times and error rates to ensure that the new system is working effectively.
- Finally, the library would establish metrics to measure the success or failure of their improvement initiatives, such as a reduction in the average time it takes to locate and retrieve a digital asset or a decrease in the number of errors encountered.

By continuously monitoring and improving their digital asset management process, the library can ensure that their information governance project is successful and provides value to the organization.

It is critical to be able to establish metrics to measure the success or failure of improvement initiatives. Four key qualitative and quantitative metrics for improvement include risk, efficiency, quality, and patron satisfaction. Risk tends to be more qualitative in nature but might be measured and extrapolated—compared to previous years—as a reduction in legal actions, regulatory fines, data remediations, or data breaches. Efficiency is generally a measure of time, for example, decreasing the average duration to process a reference request or interlibrary loan. That reduction in processing time will not only create opportunity for additional value-added activities but also likely make for greater patron satisfaction since they have more time to engage with library resources.

Quality of a service can often be measured as a reduction in errors, complaints, calls, or returns. Patron satisfaction can be evaluated with internal or external surveys, as well as positive or negative reviews on social media.

Several use cases for continuous improvement in a library include:

- *Process improvement*: Identification of inefficiencies in a process and implementing changes to make the process more efficient. This can include eliminating nonvalue-added steps or automating manual processes.
- *Quality improvement*: Diagnosis of defects in a product or service and implementing changes to reduce or eliminate

those defects, ultimately improving the quality of the product or service.

- *Employee engagement*: Improvement of employee engagement by providing opportunities for employees to contribute ideas and feedback and by recognizing and rewarding employees who make significant contributions to the library.
- *Customer experience*: Improvement of patron experience by identifying pain points in the patron's usage of library systems and implementing changes to address those pain points, ultimately improving customer satisfaction and loyalty.
- *Risk management*: Identification and mitigation of risks within a library by identifying potential risks and implementing changes to reduce the likelihood or impact of those risks.
- *Innovation*: Fostering a culture of innovation within a library by encouraging employees to think creatively and to suggest new ideas for improving products, services, or processes.

CHAPTER 20

KPIs and Metrics

The purpose of using and deploying project metrics is to provide meaningful quantitative proofs required to answer important questions or hypotheses about improved or degraded performance. As such, it is comparative in nature and speaks to material changes in performance or relationships. GIGO (garbage in/out) is an example of poor inputs, which lead to poor outputs or conclusions. Poor conclusions also lead to faulty and consequential organization decisions. So, it is not enough to have metrics; they must be meaningful and accurate and answer specific questions or hypotheses.

Without using metrics in a library-based information governance project, everything becomes guesswork, and the stakes are too high to leave outcomes to chance. When senior managers ask for reports, they are not particularly interested in feelings or opinions—unless they are informed by data. They also need to understand what specific conclusions can be drawn: for example, whether a new process or technology is helping the library get better, faster, or more efficient; or whether operations can establish a particular baseline responding to tier 3 escalations within a certain timeframe that is equal to or less than industry standards.

Metrics tend to be both commonplace and unique—common in the sense that virtually no pursuit is above or beyond our ability to represent it quantitatively, and unique in the sense that, while libraries have distinct similarities, each library is structured differently enough as to frame different questions.

Because different interacting groups interact to pose very distinctive questions, successful support requests or total resources produced are reasonably straightforward. But specific bugs, issues, or errors are likely to be more complicated. Thus, the question is how to build or identify quality metrics, which are reliable, repeatable, and help facilitate decision making, which has the highest probability of accuracy and success.

In certain cases, the question may be more qualitative than quantitative, for example, less a matter of operational efficiency than reducing risk. Even so, one can still require metrics that are either precise or serve as reasonably reliable indicators, for example, fewer data remediations or process errors.

Of course, metrics need not trend in a positive direction. A negative correlation, for example, exists between error and efficiency. Imagine a library production line where human beings were replaced with robots. We should expect to see an inverse relationship where errors are significantly decreased, which leads to a significant increase in production, as well as a simultaneous reduction in cost per item over time. Negative correlations are often more useful in terms of identifying and isolating waste or bottlenecks so they can be systematically pinpointed and eliminated.

Not only should metrics tell us what is working and not working, but they should also be coupled with strategic goals and objectives. It could be, for example, that a change in process or technology has a predictably adverse impact in the short term due to scale, integration, or training but appears to suggest greater strategic gains over the medium or long term. Leadership needs to be able to track progress or expose problems so they can be accurately identified, managed, and corrected.

At the same time, a poorly framed question or hypothetical, which fails to properly isolate variables, can render metrics useless or provide more confusion than clarity. In our example of library robotics, we might find that we are, in fact, producing more items but at a higher cost. Or conversely, reducing human error but decreasing production output. So, "are the robots helping us produce more items?" does not properly contextualize whether we are not only more productive but also more efficient. Better questions might be what our current costs per item are with the new technology and whether trendlines confirm reductions over particular time periods that agree with expectations. That would likely answer the question, for example, as to whether the percentage of item recalls is being reduced because of that new technology.

When undertaking information governance implementation projects, metrics are a vital component for providing insights into where an organization should commit resources. Not only do these metrics allow senior managers to make informed decisions, but they also carry the risk of opportunity cost, or the loss of comparative benefits that could have been achieved from alternative decisions. Therefore, it is crucial to monitor and report on key performance indicators (KPIs) regularly. The SMART acronym, which stands for specific, measurable, achievable, realistic, and timely, is also useful for setting goals that align with the organization's objectives. Risk response planning and analysis are also important for framing what-if scenarios that can be used if unexpected circumstances arise.

Good data is critical for making informed decisions, but the data must be fit for the purpose. Although operational metrics for information governance may differ from those in other areas, their purpose is essentially the same: to reflect the truthful status of performance over time. Metrics must be reviewed retrospectively over time, depending on the nature and complexity of the question being asked. Starting a project with limited metrics and improving them over time is a common approach.

Vendors are becoming more responsive to their clients' needs in terms of providing actionable metrics, and organizations are seeking to minimize inefficient gathering and presentation of performance indicators. It is important to provide accurate data and insights to senior management, but it can create unnecessary work and effort if not executed correctly or if failing to utilize tools that are commonly available in the market. It is always best to generate data that is as close to a real-time snapshot as possible, unless the data is retrospective, and time is of less importance.

Given are several fact patterns illustrating the earlier concepts:

A library is implementing a new information governance policy to comply with new privacy regulations. They set a goal to have all staff trained on the new policy within three months. They measure progress by tracking how many staff members have completed the training each week and comparing it to their target. They realize that they are not on track to meet their goal and adjust their approach by providing additional training sessions and resources. By monitoring their progress using specific and measurable metrics, they are able to make adjustments and ultimately achieve their goal in four months.

A library is implementing a new system for managing digital records. They set a goal to migrate all existing records to the new system within six months. They regularly track progress by measuring the volume of records migrated each day, identifying bottlenecks in the process and adjusting their approach to overcome them. They also use risk response planning and analysis to identify potential problems and develop contingency plans in case they arise. By using operational metrics that are fit for the purpose and regularly monitoring progress, they are able to successfully migrate all records within the six-month timeframe.

A library is working with a vendor to implement a new system for managing patron data. The vendor provides regular metrics on system performance, but the library staff find the data overwhelming and difficult to analyze. They develop a more streamlined approach by identifying KPIs that are most relevant to their goals and objectives. They also adopt tools and products that are commonly available in the market to help with data analysis and presentation. By focusing on the metrics that are most important to their project and using the right tools to manage and analyze the data, they are able to get more useful insights and make better decisions.

CHAPTER 21

Knowledge Management

In the context of information governance project management for libraries, knowledge management is a critical discipline that can help libraries capture, organize, and leverage their collective knowledge and information. A library's knowledge base is its greatest asset, and it is essential that this knowledge be formally captured, organized, and made easily accessible to library staff.

Technology has revolutionized knowledge management, making it easier to organize and extract information that would otherwise be lost or underutilized. However, the success of knowledge management in a library will depend on the effort put into creating and maintaining a useful, easy-to-use knowledge base.

Creating an effective knowledge management system requires a framework that reflects the library's culture, which starts at the top. The challenges of creating a useful knowledge base include capturing information in a format that is useful and educational, keeping it up-to-date, and finding the time and incentive to invest in knowledge management.

Assuming a library can overcome these challenges and create an effective knowledge management system, there are numerous benefits. Sharing information promotes a culture that supports employees while serving the library's goals. Employees who feel invested in and supported are more likely to be motivated, collaborate more effectively, and contribute to the library's success. Cross-training is another example of knowledge sharing that can help build redundancy and promote understanding between library teams.

With the right framework and tools in place, a library can leverage its collective knowledge and information to maximize redundancy, secure its prospects over time, and contribute to the growth and success of the organization.

Given are two fact patterns illustrating the importance of knowledge management in information governance project management for libraries:

A library has a large number of digital collections that are maintained by different departments within the organization. However, there is no centralized knowledge management system in place to organize and share information about these collections. As a result, when a librarian wants to locate a particular collection, they must ask their colleagues for assistance. This leads to inefficiencies and missed opportunities for the library, as librarians spend time searching for information instead of providing assistance to patrons. In addition, the library risks losing valuable institutional knowledge when librarians retire or move on to other organizations, as their knowledge about the collections is not formally documented and shared.

A library has a small team of catalogers who are responsible for managing the library's catalog. However, each cataloger has their own way of cataloging items, leading to inconsistencies in the catalog and making it difficult for patrons to find what they are looking for. The library realizes the need for a centralized knowledge management system to standardize cataloging procedures and improve the accuracy and consistency of the catalog. By implementing a knowledge management system, the library is able to document and share cataloging procedures, allowing all catalogers to access the same information and ensure consistency across the catalog. This results in a more user-friendly catalog and better service for library patrons.

CHAPTER 22

Compliance and Risk Management

In libraries and library systems, compliance and governance collaborate in an interdependent relationship. Compliance frameworks establish safeguards and controls to meet legal, regulatory, and industry certification requirements while governance provides strategic direction and oversight. Compliance staff must have a full grasp of technology and how it aligns with the strategic goals of the organization.

Risk assessments and audits are a regular feature in compliance. Standards and requirements are also industry-specific, sometimes requiring infrastructure, process, rules, and retention requirements. For libraries, some of the critical compliance standards include privacy and confidentiality, accessibility, copyright, and licensing requirements.

These assessments should meet ISO standards. For example, failing to meet compliance standards can have significant consequences, including reputational damage and loss of trust among patrons and stakeholders, such as the research community and potential research data subjects. Compliance must start at the top and sensitize employees to the consequences so that it becomes ingrained in the organizational culture and practices. Providing relevant training and education is critical to keep employees up-to-date on changing regulations and best practices. Compliance requires stringent practices around maintaining documentation for reporting purposes, general defensibility, and prospective audits and investigations.

Compliance staff must work closely with IT auditors and risk managers, critical functions in libraries and library systems. Their role should be to identify and eliminate material hazards, which might pose an obstacle to realizing operational goals that are tied to strategic organizational goals.

IT audits and assessments serve as a first step in interrogating controls and measuring and quantifying.

It is, however, unfortunately, all too common for libraries to discover risks and vulnerabilities in their information governance practices only after the fact. Therefore, it is highly recommended that their onboarding processes go beyond mere software vulnerability scanning to identify potential issues.

One common challenge for libraries is managing communications stored in organizational applications, particularly data that falls under regulatory retention requirements. To address this, a protocol should be established to retain or destroy such data as appropriate. In many cases, data can be moved to an archive and destroyed in its native application, or it may be left unused on an application due to a lack of migration protocol.

To ensure that governance practices and guidelines remain effective, they must be codified across IT while also remaining adaptable and usable by other important staff stakeholders. While it is important to tailor programs to specific groups, regions, or countries, it's essential to ensure that strategic goals remain aligned and consistent across the organization.

A successful information governance program must establish and enforce the fundamentals of governance and compliance across all relevant IT stakeholders. This includes addressing potential technical and operational difficulties that may arise if infrastructure, systems, and software applications lack proper interoperability. Third-party audits should also be conducted during the onboarding, RFP, and proof-of-concept phases to ensure that the program remains effective and aligned with best practices.

In addition, library management must use compliance principles to ensure that IT audits are not complicated by avoidable harms, particularly because people are prone to error, inconsistency, ego, and territoriality. Effective auditors should, in particular, conduct interviews, not interrogations, and rely heavily on subject matter experts who are more familiar with day-to-day processes and operations.

Given are two fact patterns illustrating the aforementioned principles.

A library's board of trustees has decided to implement an information governance project to improve the management of patron data. During the onboarding process, the library's IT department performs a software vulnerability scan of the existing library management system and discovers that the system is not compliant with certain regulatory retention requirements. To address this issue, the IT department develops a protocol for retaining or destroying data based on regulatory requirements and implements a migration protocol to move data to an archive and destroy it in the native application. During a third-party audit of the library's information governance practices, the auditor asks about the retention protocol and migration protocol, and the library is able to provide evidence of compliance.

A library director has implemented an information governance project to address the risks associated with unstructured data stored in shared drives across the library's various departments. The IT department has developed governance practices and guidelines for managing the shared drives, but has allowed for some flexibility to accommodate the needs of individual departments. However, during a review of the project, it becomes clear that some departments are not following the established governance practices and are storing sensitive data in unsecured folders. Additionally, the shared drives lack proper interoperability, causing difficulties for departments that need to collaborate across different drives. To address these issues, the library director establishes and enforces governance fundamentals across all departments and requires compliance with the established governance practices. The IT department also develops a plan to improve interoperability among the shared drives to improve collaboration and reduce the risk of data breaches.

CHAPTER 23

Operations Management

Once a library establishes an information governance vision and strategy, it stands to reason that operations must then provide expertise on the best way to convert and execute that vision to be successful. This leads to a more grounded technical perspective on how best to achieve it as effectively, efficiently, and economically as possible. But again, where leadership should develop a vision that extends just beyond the event horizon of what is possible, technology must keep its feet planted on the ground, though not too firmly as to lose sight of opportunities or avenues for innovation and improvement.

IT operations can be extraordinarily complicated, involving the coordination of dozens of critical areas, which together ensure that hundreds, if not thousands, of systems, servers, archives, applications, and processes that ensure organizational success have *near perfect* uptimes. And in the case of inevitable breakdowns or interruptions, a detailed and tested organizational continuity plan is in place to recover from virtually any contingency as quickly as possible. Thus, a vision to one may appear more like formal requirements to another; especially one who must leverage technology to bring it to life. Ideas become material and tactile and have moving parts, people, and processes that must work together within the laws of physics to get as close to that vision as possible. To that end, strong operations teams look for the most reliable, forward-thinking ways to solve problems and favorably position their organization relative to competition, using the finite resources at their disposal in terms of finance, teams, or technology. Organizations with a robust vision, often though not exclusively in technology, focus on effective and innovative research and development apparatuses, which can deliver the best of both worlds; speed and stability to market while working out technical advances and improvements in a development setting with the hope of gaining a competitive edge against competitors over time.

Operations essentially operate within the enterprise like an organization responsible for implementing and supporting IT services. Thus, the various departments they support, despite working in the same organization, can be considered clients or customers. So, it is crucial to establish reliable frameworks to manage those challenges while at the same time ensuring they align with the organization's strategic objectives. It is equally crucial to build trusting, collaborative relationships that will put all the key stakeholders in a position to be successful, which in turn bodes well for the overall success of the organization. Unfortunately, it is not unusual for different departments within the same organization to develop antagonistic relationships, especially in the absence of strong leadership. This is often the case between budget staff members and technology, oftentimes exacerbated by a combination of crises and unrealistic expectations. SLAs are important, of course, but no more so than committing to amicable relationships from the top down.

Operations will also regularly engage in assessing new technology, from product demonstrations through increasingly formal reviews, starting with RFIs (requests for information) or RFPs (requests for proposal). In most organizations, an RFI will accompany a demonstration of a product or service in order to graduate a vendor into a more thorough and formal queue of vendors to be considered for an RFP. Depending on the complexity of the system or platform and the necessity to the organization, an RFP can stretch from months to years. In smaller organizations, or if a system is either less complex or deemed to pose only moderate risk, an RFI and RFP might be interchangeable. Or in fact, it might be more cost effective for an organization to simply buy a product without investing precious time and resources in an RFP process. There are also exceptions where a software or Software as a Service (SaaS) platform is a known entity, and a formal evaluation either can be accelerated or is largely unnecessary.

Whatever the size of the organization, any significant investment in terms of time and capital should follow proper procurement protocols. Most medium to large enterprises have a dedicated procurement function to do just that. They will coordinate with stakeholders on timelines, vendor outreach and management, negotiating pricing and payment terms, and working with legal and operations to finalize agreements, deliverables, and SLAs. Again, the process for a formal selection and negotiating an agreement could take weeks or drag on for months.

Operation's purview will also include training, supporting, and monitoring organizational applications; testing and implementing software installations, upgrades, or enhancements; improving, automating, and documenting processes; supporting, escalating, and investigating technical issues; coordinating and negotiating with third-party vendors; building policies and procedures; and reporting on SLAs, metrics, and KPIs. With all the moving parts within large technical operations management teams, along with the pressure to maintain operational excellence, it is necessary to establish formal guidelines or frameworks to maintain structure and order. Two such popular, and often overlapping, frameworks include COBIT (Control Objectives for Information and Related Technologies) and ITIL (IT Infrastructure Library). The COBIT framework was developed by ISACA (Information Systems Audit and Control Association), which takes a broad, holistic approach to governance and is also known for its various IT trainings and certifications across audit, risk, enterprise management, privacy, and security.

At a high level, the COBIT goals or principles are meant to align stakeholder needs; provide consistent governance across the entire organization; employ a single, unified framework; ensure a holistic approach; and distinguish between the goals of management and the strategic governance team. A simple way to understand the difference is between strategy and tactics. The senior governance team establishes and monitors objectives, and the management builds and executes the plans to achieve those objectives. Imagine a battlefield on which the cavalry takes advantage of a seemingly obvious tactical opportunity only to unwittingly thwart an artillery barrage, along with the strategic initiative. Therefore, it is vital to align strategic objectives and effectively communicate them across the entire organization.

Where COBIT is broader and focused on strategic governance across the entire organization, ITIL operates exclusively within the domain of IT, concentrating on planning, process, best practice, and continuous improvement. But the principles and frameworks are meant to compliment rather than compete against one another. In fact, COBIT states this quite clearly and includes a number of other standards, including

TOGAF and ISO. TOGAF stands for The Open Group Architecture Forum and, as its name implies, is principally concerned with enterprise architecture. ISO (International Organization for Standardization) is a nongovernmental organization that extends well beyond governance and information technology and security.

The five formal stages in the ITIL framework include service strategy, design, transition, operation, and improvement. Service strategy is concentrated on how to implement and sustain effective client service, which will involve sustained collaboration with appropriate governance committees. Service design advances strategy by converting it into what is tangible and achievable, either for the purpose of improving current offerings or for introducing new offerings. This will involve close cooperation with various entities, not to mention stakeholders in infrastructure, architecture, and asset management. Service transition ensures assets are interoperable and vigorously stress-tested prior to introducing new or improved systems or services through the change management process. This will very often involve working intimately with third-party vendors and must also account for potential rollbacks or any issues which could impact availability and user access management.

Service operation focuses on serving clients or entities according to previously negotiated SLAs and delivery objectives and includes hands-on support, training, monitoring, incident management, issues reporting, capacity management, escalations, and remediations. With an array of constant challenges and emergencies, prioritization is crucial, as well as coordinating with governance stakeholders and ensuring excellent communication protocols. This will better ensure that proper controls are in place to safeguard compliance and reduce risk exposure. Finally, through metrics, KPIs, and analysis, continuous service improvement applies the lessons of the previous stages to constantly and incrementally make the service more efficient and economical, while improving data and organizational intelligence—not as a single, static point in time but as ongoing policy, procedure, and principle.

Given next are several examples of how libraries can deploy the COBIT and ITIL frameworks to improve the likelihood of their information governance implementation project success:

A library is planning to implement a new system for managing and preserving digital archives. The library's IT team decides to use the COBIT framework to ensure that the project is aligned with the library's overall goals and objectives. They begin by identifying the key stakeholders and defining the scope of the project. Then, they create a governance plan that outlines the roles and responsibilities of each stakeholder and sets up a communication plan. The IT team uses COBIT's assessment and audit capabilities to continuously monitor and evaluate the project's progress and make necessary adjustments.

A local library system has been struggling with data quality issues and decides to implement an ITIL-based information governance program. The library system's IT team begins by defining the library's business objectives and identifying the IT services that are necessary to achieve those objectives. They then establish a data quality management program that includes data profiling, cleansing, and enrichment. They also set up a data governance framework that includes data ownership, data classification, and data life cycle management. The IT team uses ITIL's service management capabilities to ensure that the information governance program is aligned with the library's overall service management strategy.

An academic research library is planning to migrate its data from an on-premise system to the cloud. The library's IT team decides to use a combination of COBIT and ITIL to ensure that the migration is successful. They begin by using COBIT's governance and management practices to define the project's scope and goals. Then, they use ITIL's service management practices to plan the migration, including identifying the necessary IT services, establishing SLAs, and defining the change management process. They use COBIT's assessment and audit capabilities to continuously monitor the migration and ensure that it is aligned with the library's overall goals and objectives.

CHAPTER 24

Incident Management

Incident management focuses on identifying and minimizing the impact of unanticipated events that may have a significantly disruptive impact on operations and then restoring those operations to a functional state as quickly as possible. The incident management life cycle consists of five stages, which include planning, detection, containment, postmortem, and closure. Planning requires building an incident response team (IRT) in tandem with policies, training, checklists, and a communication plan. The detection phase defines the priority and type of incidents, along with monitoring tools that help prevent, detect, and circulate notifications. The containment phase tactically executes the previous planning and detection phases, probes and documents the nature of the incident, and initializes recovery procedures. The postmortem phase is essentially a well-documented lessons-learned exercise, which covers all the details and metrics of the incident, how well the IRT executed the recovery plan, and what needs to be done to prevent it from reoccurring. Last of all, documentation will be finalized and submitted to senior management for closure.

An impact or root cause analysis should outline in exacting terms why, where, and when an incident occurred to advice on how a solution can both fix the problem and prevent it from reoccurring. It will require teamwork between key technical stakeholders to get a full scope of the problem and all the organizations, systems, or individuals who may have been cross-impacted. The potential for legal exposure is also significant, so meticulous analysis and documentation is critical, along with guidance from legal, compliance, and senior management.

The response must also have a proper communication plan to ensure that those who have been affected have the information they need to manage any potential liability. This last point is of vital importance. In the context of a large research library, for example, senior management may have to report material issues to executive management or the parent institution's General Counsel's office, who may in turn be required to make representations to regulators, particularly if the organization is temporarily out of compliance. The remediation plan must also be reviewed and approved by management to prioritize a response, especially if there are competing priorities. Incidents can include anything from physical system failures and security breaches to data spoliation and destruction.

Incident management inevitably leads to change management where a formal, documented request outlines the reasons for the change, the solution or workaround developed by operations, the testing and validation demonstrating its feasibility, and finally, the authorization from senior or executive management. It is also important that changes are specific and well documented. Of course, management may deny a change request for any number of reasons or propose modifications or improvements. In that case, those modifications must face the same rigorous testing and validation life cycle before they can be approved and implemented.

In most cases, a change should also include a proper backout plan. For a variety of reasons, what works in a development environment should but does not always translate into a live environment. So, whether the changes are software upgrades, patches, workarounds, or structural changes, operations must be prepared to restore the system to a point in time when it was operational. Finally, once the changes have been implemented, they must be carefully monitored and their status reported to management on a periodic basis, which will vary depending on their criticality.

The following fact patterns illustrate the aforementioned principles as applied to the context of library information governance management.

Fact Pattern 1: Large Research Library Incident Management

A large research library with several branches nationwide recently deployed an incident management system to ensure business continuity in the event of any disruptions to its operations. The library's incident management life cycle consists of five stages, starting with planning and ending with closure. The library built an IRT comprising representatives from each branch, and they developed policies, training, checklists, and a communication plan.

The detection phase is crucial for the library, as it deals with prioritizing and classifying incidents. The library has monitoring tools in place that can detect anomalies and alert the IRT when necessary. The containment phase follows the detection phase, and it involves executing the plan developed during the planning phase, documenting the incident's nature, and beginning recovery procedures.

The library also conducts a postmortem phase after an incident to identify the root cause of the problem and determine how to prevent it from happening again. The documentation produced in the postmortem phase is shared with senior management and submitted for closure.

Recently, the library faced a cybersecurity incident that affected several branches. The IRT immediately implemented the incident response plan, containing the incident and minimizing the impact on the library's operations. The IRT conducted a root cause analysis, identified the cause of the incident, and proposed remediation steps to prevent a recurrence.

The library's communication plan ensured that all affected parties were informed and had access to the necessary information to manage any potential liability. Senior management approved the remediation plan, and the changes were carefully monitored and reported periodically.

Fact Pattern 2: Library System Failure Incident Management

A large library system comprising several libraries across a state recently implemented an incident management system to manage and minimize the impact of unanticipated events that may have a significantly disruptive effect on operations. The library system's incident management life cycle consists of planning, detection, containment, postmortem, and closure.

The library system built an IRT, developed policies, training, checklists, and a communication plan. The detection phase involves classifying the incidents' priority and type, and the library system has monitoring tools in place to prevent, detect, and notify the IRT of any anomalies.

Recently, a system failure incident occurred that affected all the libraries in the system. The IRT immediately implemented the incident response plan, containing the incident and minimizing the impact on the library system's operations. The IRT conducted an impact analysis, identified the root cause of the incident, and proposed remediation steps.

The library system's communication plan ensured that all affected parties were informed and had access to the necessary information to manage any potential liability. Senior management approved the remediation plan, and the changes were carefully monitored and reported periodically.

The incident led to a change management request, which outlined the reasons for the change, the solution developed by operations, and the testing and validation demonstrating its feasibility. The change request was authorized by senior management, and a proper backout plan was developed in case the changes did not work as intended. The changes were carefully monitored and periodically reported to senior management.

CHAPTER 25

Organizational Continuity

Successful organizational continuity planning and preparedness is measured by an organization's ability to maintain or restore business-as-usual operations during a major disruption. That includes resiliency for virtually any type of natural or unnatural disaster that could impact operations, including branch locations, data centers, systems, third-party systems, or infrastructure on which the library relies for critical functions.

The adoption of remote technology during the COVID pandemic is an example of a process and technology adjustment, which more or less maintained most business-as-usual operations in an efficient, cost-effective manner. A more critical and challenging example would be a document management or archiving system crashing, or actually being destroyed, that would suddenly make data unavailable to the library and its stakeholders, and thus, render the organization unable to service its employees or users.

A library's organizational continuity model must first establish its strategic objectives. That starts with alignment across the organization as well as identifying and interviewing key stakeholders such as managers, employees, teams, and third parties. Roles must be understood and established along with any required training or individual action plans, for example, where members of the team would physically locate if their regular location became inaccessible. Due to the potential complications, many organizations maintain a formal organizational continuity management function, which includes a manager to coordinate activities and manage communications and a team of organizational continuity specialists to support those efforts.

The first priority in applying organizational continuity standards is to conduct and document a thorough risk assessment. This will include identifying, classifying, and quantifying the level of risk to locations, technology, data, utilities, inventory, or third parties. Each will then require an understanding as to whether or to what degree they are mission-critical and what constitutes acceptable levels of reduced output or production. Next, the organizational continuity team should work with key organizational units to design, document, and implement a resiliency plan, which accounts for those acceptable levels of reduced service during the recovery, as well as the underlying systems and applications that support them. The plan must outline specific and appropriate recovery time objectives (RTO), or the length of time it takes to restore organizational processes, and recovery point objectives (RPO), or the amount of data that can be lost during the recovery phase.

The resiliency plan must also include a detailed communication plan, which identifies and enumerates all of the library's or library system's key stakeholders and who must be reported to and updated on a regular basis during a disruption, internally and externally. The details of the reporting will naturally vary depending on the roles of the recipients. A regulator or researcher is highly unlikely to see the same unexpurgated information as senior management. The communication plan will often include legal, compliance, public relations, and other important internal stakeholder departments.

In addition to identifying areas of vulnerability, a resiliency plan must consider the specific data and information that may be compromised, not just temporarily but permanently. Thus, it is critical to establish a data map, which includes critical or sensitive information, along with appropriate backup and recovery so that data can be secured and recovered. That data might include sensitive financial records, intellectual property, or customer information, and hard copy data as well as digital. Finally, testing and validation must be coordinated with audit departments or groups and conducted on a regular periodic basis to ensure that planning and readiness work under disaster conditions. For example, if a data site was actually destroyed and all systems were shut down, a failover should kick in so that all key data is recoverable and available to the organization remotely from an alternative, mirrored data center.

The given fact pattern illustrates how these principles can be applied in the context of a large research library.

The subject research library is one of the largest in the country, with multiple branches and a vast collection of books, journals, and digital resources. The library serves a diverse community of users, including students, faculty, researchers, and members of the public.

The library has a comprehensive organizational continuity plan in place, which is regularly reviewed and updated by a team of organizational continuity specialists. The plan covers a wide range of potential disruptions, including natural disasters, cyberattacks, system failures, and other events that could impact the library's operations.

As part of the plan, the library has conducted a thorough risk assessment, which has identified the most critical areas of vulnerability. These include the library's data centers, which host the library's digital resources, as well as the physical locations of the branches and the inventory of books and journals. The library has established specific RTO and RPO for each critical system and application. For example, the RTO for restoring the library's website is two hours, while the RPO for the library's financial records is zero, meaning that no data loss is acceptable.

The library has also developed a detailed communication plan, which outlines the roles and responsibilities of key stakeholders during a disruption. The plan includes regular updates to senior management, employees, third-party vendors, and other internal and external stakeholders. The library has identified the most effective communication channels for each group, such as e-mail, phone, text message, or social media. The library has also established a data map, which identifies the critical or sensitive information that may be compromised during a disruption. The map includes both digital and hard copy data, such as financial records, intellectual property, and customer information. The library has implemented appropriate backup and recovery procedures for each type of data, which ensure that data can be secured and recovered in a timely and efficient manner.

Finally, the library regularly tests and validates its organizational continuity plan to ensure that it is effective under disaster conditions. The library conducts regular drills and simulations, which involve shutting down critical systems and applications and testing the failover to alternative data centers. The library also works closely with audit departments to ensure that its planning and readiness meet regulatory and compliance requirements.

CHAPTER 26

Data Mapping and Classification

Best Practices for Record Capturing[1]

Generally, to "capture" means to place records (or data) that an organization has created into an information management system and to record the existence of such records into the system.[2]

According to ISO 15489, capturing has three essential purposes:

- Establishing a relationship between the record, the creator, and the business context that originated it—and ensuring that the records are trustworthy, reliable, and authentic. As a result, it is critical to capture a record in its context as close to the event it documents as possible (a significant portion of that context is captured in the form of metadata).
- Ensuring that the record is placed into a controlled environment—and, specifically, protecting the record and its metadata from alteration, tampering, or even accidental deletion, in a manner that helps to demonstrate its trustworthiness and authenticity.
- Creating a link between the captured record to other related records. for example, all personnel files, so as to enable such files to be managed in a similar fashion.[3]

---

[1] Capturing information | naa.gov.au.
[2] What is Information Capture? Definition, Purpose, and Value (aiim.org).
[3] Id.

In addition, according to the Association for Intelligent Information Management (AIIM), there are a number of other core reasons for capturing documents that support business goals and objectives:

- Enabling innovation by centralizing access to information and allowing personnel to know that the version they have is correct, current, and approved: Most approaches to capture result in some centralization of access.
- Enriching customer and system-user experience—capture allows system users and customers to know where documents are and that they are complete and correct and enables customer service staff to respond to queries efficiently and effectively, for example, via a self-service website, portal, or mobile app.
- Minimizing risk and protecting data assets—for example, by deploying access controls to ensure that only authorized individuals have access to digital assets and only to the ones they should have access to. This is much easier to do when documents are stored in a secure repository. Libraries can also set up security to ensure that documents cannot be printed, downloaded, or e-mailed outside the organization. In addition, following document capture, the system administrator can configure the system to ensure that the document may not be modified or deleted (other than in specific circumstances) so as to promote reliance on authentic records.[4]

Based on these criteria, the essential part of managing a library or other agency's business information and records is to capture it into systems that manage and support its use over time.[5]

The list outlines some of the core information governance best practices for capturing institutional (including library) documents:

- Make the capture process easy for all staff. This should reduce the risk of information and records not being captured.

---

[4] Id.
[5] Capturing information | naa.gov.au.

- Where possible:
    - Automate the capturing process.
    - Integrate capture into normal business processes.
    - Provide clear, precise instructions and support—in particular, it is critical for staff to know where staff must capture information and to instruct them not to keep business records on personal drives including shared drives or on group work spaces; examples can include:
        - Electronic document and records management systems (EDRMS).
        - Administration systems for finance and human resources management.
        - Paper registry files.
- Digitize physical records—physical records (such as paper documents, photographs, or audiovisual material) can deteriorate over time which be both costly and risky. Best practices include:
    - Scanning incoming correspondence so it can be managed more effectively through the workflow.
    - Clearly identifying what paper is being received.
    - Itemizing which business processes are linked to or reliant on the paper.
    - Determining whether scanning the paper will improve the business process by making it faster, more efficient, less resource intensive, the costs and risks of maintaining the paper document, and the costs and risks of digitization with its likely benefits.

Why Is Data Mapping Important?

Data mapping informs how data is stored, moved, searched, and accessed throughout the enterprise. This has great implications for operations, governance, data privacy, and organizational intelligence. A data map should also demonstrate which systems are on or off grid, when they became active or inactive, what function they serve, why they are strategically or tactically relevant, where they are located, and the level of their interoperability.

Data mapping is also essential to the governance and information security management principle of CIA (confidentiality, integrity, and availability). Confidentiality speaks to the need to designate data by sensitivity and restrict user access. Integrity refers to preventing the willful or accidental deletion or modification of data. And availability ensures that data is appropriately and effectively available to those who have the rights to access and modify it.

Data mapping is particularly important in the context of privacy compliance. For example, the effective use of data mapping can help a research library to identify and track where personal data resides, especially for cross-border transfers and data subject access requests, which can be critical when managing the personal data of data subjects who reside in jurisdictions with comprehensive privacy laws. In this context, the data subject might also request additional information for which the enterprise is responsible, such as validating their data was processed; details as to how and where the data was obtained; and relevant details if decisions were part of an automated decision-making process.

There are many challenges to building and maintaining an accurate data map, which is essential to data life cycle management, particularly for organizations such as libraries that manage large volumes of diverse data. With data systems and sources constantly in flux, they are difficult to keep current. A manual approach is particularly laborious and inefficient and often subject to inaccuracy or incompleteness, for example, inconsistencies in metadata between targets and sources, which could lead to over- or underretention; keeping what has outlived its legal or organizational usefulness; or destroying what should have been preserved. A poor data map also undermines an organization's ability to migrate, consolidate, or enhance metadata, which in turn undercuts its ability for optimized search and analysis, both of which are vital to building and extracting organizational intelligence.

Data mapping starts with teamwork and cooperating with key stakeholders and subject matter experts to inventory and identify all key data assets and their utility to an organization, from e-mail, archiving, and messaging systems, to backups and document management systems. Advances in technology have made it easier to scan and automate significant aspects of the mapping process and are highly recommended. But at the same time, many are off grid or third-party systems, which require more than the presumption of a few keystrokes. Metadata must consistently track across systems and searches. And automated or not, validation and testing is essential. In the process of how data is modified and retained during its life cycle, a quality data map can help better identify areas of improvement, such as eliminating duplicative systems, archives, databases, or processes and consolidating or rerouting them for greater efficiency.

A data map also positions the enterprise for next-level improvements in data classification, which can be defined as the process of categorizing structured, unstructured, or semistructured data based on sensitivity, file type, or any number of taxonomies useful to the enterprise. In general, the first use case for classification is assigning levels of sensitivity or confidentiality to minimize risk. But it can also be used for applying retention schedules, maintaining data privacy requirements (such as limiting access to personally identifiable information or personal data), or extracting analytics and organizational intelligence. Operationally, a proactive data classification program offers a number of benefits, including consolidation, improved metrics and analytics, and more efficient means of destroying ROT or obsolescent data.

Depending on the data, architecture, scale, and technology, classification can be implemented manually or automatically, or just as often, as hybrid. Manual classification has the benefit of enhanced user input, particularly on the subjective matter of security and sensitivity, but it is also slow and inconsistent. Automated classification tools have been improving in recent years but can choke out on large data sets or produce false positives. And chunking out data into smaller, more manageable sets improves performance but limits scalability. Though their setup time can also be significant, it is generally worth the effort.

Some platforms offer what is referred to as visual classification, which is an automated process for categorizing images or data based on matching visual attributes. Both are challenged with the ability to scale, whether the data sits in one massive archive or a more distributed architecture. It is crucial to establish a consistent and strategic data classification program across the enterprise; outline consistent rules; understand the scope and limitations of a platform; and regularly audit, test, validate, and improve on the results over time.

What follows next are two fact patterns illustrating the importance and utility of data mapping in the context of library information governance management.

Fact Pattern 1—Local Library System

A local library system in New Jersey has recently undertaken an information governance project to ensure that it complies with all privacy laws and regulations. As part of this project, they have decided to conduct a data mapping exercise to identify all the personal data they hold, where it is located, how it is used, and who has access to it.

The library system has several branches, and they all maintain their own databases of patron information, including names, addresses, phone numbers, and borrowing history. The central library system also maintains a database of all materials held by the library, including books, DVDs, and other media.

To conduct the data mapping exercise, the library system brought in a team of consultants who worked with key stakeholders across the organization, including IT staff, librarians, and legal counsel. Together, they identified all the databases and systems that held personal data and then mapped out the data flows and relationships between them.

They discovered that there were several areas of the library system where personal data was being collected, used, or stored that had not been previously identified. For example, some branches were keeping patron information in paper files that were not included in the library system's main databases. The data mapping exercise also helped the library system to identify areas where data security could be improved, such as by encrypting sensitive data or limiting access to certain databases.

As a result of the data mapping exercise, the library system was able to develop a comprehensive inventory of all the personal data it held and identify any areas where it was not in compliance with privacy laws and regulations. They were also able to develop policies and procedures for managing the data more effectively, including guidelines for data retention, disposal, and access controls.

Fact Pattern 2—Large Academic University

ABC University in Belgium has a large academic library that supports research across multiple disciplines, including medicine and life sciences. As part of its research activities, the university conducts clinical trials in collaboration with research partners in the European Union. Under the General Data Protection Regulation (GDPR), clinical trial data that includes personal information of EU citizens must be protected and cannot be transferred to countries outside the EU unless certain conditions are met.

ABC University is planning to transfer some of its clinical trial data to a research partner in the United States for further analysis and collaboration. However, before doing so, the university must ensure that it is in compliance with the GDPR and has appropriate safeguards in place to protect the personal information of EU citizens.

To achieve this, the university's information governance team works with its legal and compliance departments to conduct a comprehensive data mapping exercise. The team identifies all personal information that is involved in the clinical trials, including data collected from participants in the EU. They then classify the data based on its sensitivity and determine the legal basis for processing the data, which includes obtaining informed consent from participants and meeting the university's legal obligations as a research institution.

Next, the team assesses the risks associated with transferring the data to the United States and identifies appropriate safeguards that must be put in place to mitigate those risks. The team decides to implement a number of technical and organizational measures, such as encrypting the data during transmission, limiting access to the data to authorized personnel, and ensuring that the data will be used only for the specific purposes for which it was transferred.

The university's legal and compliance departments review the data mapping and risk assessment reports and approve the transfer of the clinical trial data to the United States, with appropriate safeguards in place. The university also establishes an agreement with its U.S. research partner that includes specific provisions on data protection and GDPR compliance.

By using effective data mapping and risk assessment techniques, ABC University is able to comply with its GDPR obligations and ensure the protection of personal information of EU citizens involved in its clinical trials. The university is also able to successfully implement its information governance project by creating a comprehensive framework for managing its data assets, including those involved in cross-border transfers.

Why Do Government Librarians Need an Information Management Policy?[6]

Generally, an information management policy has two main goals. First, it provides library staff with clear guidelines for creating, capturing, and managing information assets (records, information, and data) to satisfy the organization's business, legal, and stakeholder requirements. Second, it allocates responsibilities across the organization and organizational unit.

From an organizational standpoint, information management policy should align with the principles, environment, and strategic directions described in the librarian's information governance framework—and, it should be updated and developed as needed.

A defensible information management policy should have at least the following four core elements:

1. A description of the formulator's expectations for "fit-for-purposes" information management practices, processes, and systems that will support the entity's management of information as an organizational asset:
   o Examples:
     ▪ Language stating that the agency will implement fit-for-purpose information management practices and systems to ensure the creation, maintenance, and protection of reliable information and that all information management practices [in this agency] are to align this policy and its supporting procedures.
     ▪ A statement that the policy informs staff of which information assets they can routinely destroy combined

---

[6] Information governance | naa.gov.au.

with further information outlining the types of low-value and short-term information that can be destroyed in the normal course of business.

- A statement that the policy covers all business applications used to create, manage, and store information assets, including dedicated information management systems, business information systems, databases, e-mail, voice and instant messaging, websites, and social media applications.

2. A clear explanation of the benefits of good information management:
   o Examples:
     - Language stating that the purpose of the policy is to guide and direct the creation and management of information assets (records, information, and data) by staff and to clarify staff responsibilities. [The agency] is committed to establishing and maintaining information management practices that meet its business needs, accountability requirements, and stakeholder expectations.
     - Language stating that the benefit of complying with this policy include the facts that trusted information will be well described, stored in known endorsed locations, and accessible to staff and clients when needed.

3. Definitions of stakeholder and user roles and responsibilities:
   o Examples:
     - Language stating that all staff are responsible for the creation and management of information as defined by the policy followed by a separate delineation of responsibility for positions such as a chief librarian, unit managers, supervisors, and the entity's CTO.
     - Language stating that the policy applies to both permanent and contract workers.
     - A statement that managers and supervisors are responsible for ensuring staff, including contract staff, are aware of, and are supported to follow, the information management practices defined in this policy.
     - A statement within a data migration policy that describes considerations for information technology teams

migrating data from one business system to another. This may include guidance around interoperability, quality assurance testing, metadata controls, and accountable destruction of data, if all data is not being migrated.

- A note that the policy applies to all [agency] staff members and contractors and to all information assets (records, information, and data) in any format, created or received, to support [agency] business activities.
- Details on who may destroy data, which laws authorize that destruction, and how stakeholders can comply with both the library's internal procedures and applicable law when they destroy or otherwise dispose of data.

4. Alignment with the entity's commitment to meeting its business, legislative, and regulatory requirements:
   o Examples:
     - A statement that the policy is written within the context of [the agency's] information governance framework, which is located at XXXX.
     - A statement that the policy promotes the integrity and accessibility of information assets to support the delivery of business outcomes.
     - A statement that an information management policy is needed followed by an explanation of the benefits of good practice.
     - Language stating that the agency recognizes its information assets as valuable corporate assets and is committed to achieving appropriate and ongoing management of these assets to advance [the agency's] strategic priorities and meet client needs.
     - A note that all staff must take steps to protect personal information according to applicable laws and guidance including with respect to personal information stored in cloud-hosted services.

When developing a library information management policy, the formulator should also consider how it supports the entity's strategic objectives and intersects with other strategic documents.

From a design standpoint, the policy formulator should ensure that the policy is designed to best meet the size, nature, and complexity of the entity's business.

For example, while it might make sense for a smaller government library or subdivision to combine its information management policy with other governance documents, such a practice is probably inadvisable for a larger entity with more complex systems and requirement. It is also important to be mindful of when different policy statements should be directed at different audiences (based on individual needs, sophistication levels, etc., to ensure they are aware of their specific requirements).

Notwithstanding, from a best-practices standpoint, policy formulators should ensure that their target audience:

- Knows which processes, practices, and procedures should be used (and avoided) when undertaking information management tasks, including record creation, capture, and disposal
- Understands which systems are officially approved for managing information assets
- Is aware of proper record destruction practices
- Understands its various roles, responsibilities, and expectations as they relate to managing information assets
- Knows how this policy relates to other organizational policies and procedures

Given the complexity of information management for large organizations, in particular, it is likely that it will take more than one policy document to provide guidance across all processes. Information management policy statements should be embedded into a broad range of organizational policies and procedures, to assist ease of access by stakeholders. Dividing policy statements across several documents can also enhance readability by focusing on one area of information management.

Because the policy must be usable and confusion should be avoided, any policy framework implemented by a library or other organization should avoid reference to extraneous laws, directions, and requirements. An example of such a requirement could be to use a case study reference that refers to specific legislation that does not specifically apply to the intended operating environment.

Specific examples of appropriate guidance include:

- A listing of systems and locations that the library endorses for the capture and storage of information (and those which should not be used because of security concerns, etc., such as shared folders, personal drives, or external hard drives)
- Details on how information should be stored, for example, by referencing specific physical and digital record formats, security protocols, or data preservation requirements
- A description of access controls that are pertinent to the library's operating environment such as details on when it is appropriate to restrict access, when the public is entitled to access certain data based on applicable freedom of information (or similar-type) law requirements, and how the agency supports that release (and what authorizes the method of support)
- Information on when data may be transferred to a third party and on the rules governing that transfer, including specific information regarding the archiving of vital records (together with supporting guidelines, etc.)
- Guidance related to the provision of training, advice, and general staff support, including information on how information management products, tools, and systems will be acquired, developed, or implemented that includes information on the frequency of training, the duty to inform staff of their training obligations, and the necessity of providing training that is pertinent to the various groups trained.
- Language setting forth the library's commitment to regularly reviewing the policy and monitoring compliance, relevance, and continued awareness (e.g., this policy will be updated as needed if there are any changes in the business or regulatory environment. It is scheduled for a comprehensive review by 20XX. The head of the information management unit

will initiate this review and the information governance committee will conduct it.)

- A list of resources that give extra information including contact details of relevant staff within the agency, as well as useful reference material.

Finally, from a corporate governance standpoint, policy formulators should provide evidence that the appropriate officers or managers that are responsible for information management have endorsed the policy. One best practice in this respect is to include a brief paragraph signed by the relevant internal supervisory authority, recognizing the important place of information management in the agency and directing staff to comply with and monitor the policy requirements.

CHAPTER 27

Archival Standards

The preamble to ISO 17068 states, somewhat obviously, that the use of digital systems has resulted in the production of digital records, which need to be secured to ensure authenticity and legal recognition during the retention period.

However, one issue with this use is that it has given rise to an increasingly large challenge for organizations to ensure that their digital records are authentic so that they can rely on them as an effective form of evidence for important business activities over an extended period.

To address this need, a number of technology service providers have stepped into the void to provide products that promote to safeguard the authenticity, reliability, and integrity of digital records for their stated period of retention, as described in their retention schedules and similar policies.

These solutions, commonly known as trusted third-party repositories (TTPR), can offer services to identify the admissibility of clients' digital records as evidence.

A related ISO, ISO 14641-1, provides a list of criteria for determining the trustworthiness of a TTPR.

These criteria include:

- Physical security for the TTPR
- Obligations to maintain the security of the stored records
- Standards for the reliability of the repository's hardware and software systems, as well as for the user authentication and authorization and record integrity and authenticity
- Standards promoting the availability and accessibility of records

Additionally, a compliant TTPR must have policies and procedures for disaster recovery, backup, and restoration in case of system failures or other disruptions and incorporate mechanisms for the monitoring and auditing of its activities to ensure continued compliance with its policies and procedures.

The various ISO standards, provide guidelines for implementing trustworthy digital repositories. These guidelines address the necessary organizational infrastructure, digital object management, technologies, technical infrastructure, and security measures necessary for a trustworthy TTPR. One use case could be a research library implementing a digital repository to manage its collection of rare books and manuscripts. By adhering to ISO standards for TTPRs, the library can verify that the TTPR meets its needs based on an analysis of the organizational infrastructure, digital object management, and technical infrastructure in place.

In addition to the standards described earlier, most trusted TTPR providers comply with the standards established by OAIS (Open Archival Information System), which is a reference model that defines best practices for the creation, management, and preservation of digital archives. The OAIS standards have been widely adopted by many organizations responsible for creating and managing digital archives, including government agencies, research institutions, libraries, and cultural heritage institutions.

Importantly, the OAIS reference model defines specific functional requirements and responsibilities required for a compliant TTPR system, as well as a set of standards for metadata, data formats, and storage and preservation strategies. Some of the key standards and best practices associated with OAIS include:

- *Metadata standards*: OAIS defines a set of metadata standards for describing digital objects, including preservation metadata that is used to manage and preserve digital objects over time.[1] These include standards for:

---

[1] Examples of widely used digital archiving metadata standards include Dublin Core, PREMIS (PREservation Metadata: Implementation Strategies), and METS (Metadata Encoding and Transmission Standard).

- o Descriptive metadata (which describes the content and context of digital objects, and includes information such as title, author, date of creation, and keywords)
- o Administrative metadata (which provides information about how to manage and preserve digital objects, and includes information about access controls, file formats, and preservation actions that have been taken)
- o Preservation metadata (which describes the technical characteristics and preservation status of digital objects, and includes information such as checksums, fixity information, and migration history)
- *Data formats*: OAIS recommends the use of open, nonproprietary file formats that are widely supported by software and hardware platforms, that are self-describing, and that include sufficient metadata to ensure long-term access and preservation (e.g., JPEG 2000 for images, PDF/A for documents, and WAV for audio files).
- *Storage and preservation*: OAIS defines a set of guidelines for long-term storage and preservation of digital objects, including the use of redundant storage, migration of data to new formats and platforms, and fixity checks (checks to ensure that digital objects have not been corrupted or altered, and the creation of backup copies).
- *Access*: OAIS recommends that digital archives provide access to digital objects in a way that is consistent with their preservation goals and that access controls are put in place to protect the confidentiality, integrity, and availability of the digital objects.

Two examples illustrating the successful use of OAIS by research libraries are the Digital Repository Service (DRS) at the Harvard Library and the Digital Archive at the Library of Congress.

Both systems handle large amounts of data. In the case of DRS, the system supports the library's long-term management and preservation of digital objects and has successfully preserved over five million digital objects since being launched in 2005. Similarly, the Digital Archive at the Library of Congress is a massive digital repository that contains over 10 petabytes of data and has successfully preserved rare and fragile historical documents and audio recordings since its launch in the late 1990s.

To implement these goals, both systems use standards and best practices recommended by the OAIS reference model, including metadata standards; open, nonproprietary file formats; and redundant storage and backup systems.

In addition, both systems use a balance of access controls to protect the confidentiality, integrity, and availability of the digital objects while simultaneously managing the stringency of these controls against researchers' need to obtain information and to access the digital objects to perform their research.

Another important standard for libraries is TRAC (Trustworthy Repositories Audit & Certification) and is a technical report developed by the Center for Research Libraries (CRL) and the Digital Library Federation (DLF) to provide guidelines for digital repository audit and certification.

The TRAC report outlines various criteria that organizations, including libraries, can use to evaluate the success and compliance of their digital repositories and ensure that they are meeting the necessary requirements and industry best practices for long-term preservation, to facilitate access to digital information. These guidelines are broken up into three main sections: organizational infrastructure, digital object management, and technologies, technical infrastructure, and security, with each including specified criteria that must be achieved by digital repositories to achieve TRAC certification.

The organizational infrastructure section addresses the required management standards, governance structure, and policies of the repository. These include, for example, a demonstrated institutional commitment to preservation, having a clearly defined scope of collection, and providing sufficient resources.

The digital object management section addresses how organizations should create, acquire, manage, or preserve digital objects, such as implementing preservation metadata, using standardized file formats, and providing mechanisms for fixing corrupted files.

The technologies, technical Infrastructure, and security section focuses on necessary technical infrastructure and security measures, such as the use of redundant storage systems, access controls, and the regular testing and updating of security procedures.

To achieve TRAC certification, digital repositories must meet all of the criteria outlined in the TRAC report. This is accomplished through a self-assessment, followed by a third-party audit which verifies whether the repository meets the TRAC guidelines.

CHAPTER 28

ISO 19814:2017— Information and Documentation

Libraries implementing ISO/TR 19814:2017 can improve their information governance practices by delivering high-quality services that meet the needs of their communities. The standard is designed to be a guide for librarians who are responsible for managing and delivering library services. The recommendations and guidance provided in the report are based on the principles of quality management as outlined in the ISO 9000 series of standards.

Although the standard does not provide specific performance measures, it does emphasize the importance of monitoring and measuring library services to ensure that they meet the needs of users.

In addition, the standard provides guidance and recommendations related to the planning, implementation, maintenance, and improvement of the preservation of archive and library collections.

It does this through:

- Providing recommendations and guidance related to the preservation planning and ongoing management of physical collections in archives and libraries
- Listing procedures for managing collections in the stacks, research and reading rooms, conservation facilities, and while on exhibit and during transportation
- Providing guidance and recommendations for appropriate enclosures and containers for archive and library collections

The standard applies to preservation of archive and library physical collections of institutions and volumes as well as to all collections housed by a library or other relevant institution, their own proprietary collections and deposits or loans from other institutions, and certain information on digital collections. The standard also applies to collections that are being managed by governmental agencies.

At the crux of this standard is the requirement that collections intended for long-term use must be managed in a way that mitigates risks that can cause loss, including catastrophic loss from fire and floods, risks of vandalism and theft, to instability of materials, including acetate film and acidic paper.

In addition, the collections management standards set forth in this standard attempt to mitigate storage risks from a holistic perspective. Practically, this means that libraries will need to weigh the importance of various factors and create compromises based on *inter alia* the quantity and nature of collections in archives and libraries. To do this, librarians need to understand the use, significance, and vulnerability of the collections and to deploy their expertise to create best practices from several fields within the decision-making process.[1]

The core of this standard is the quality management system (QMS), which describes, how the principles of ISO/TR 19814:2017 apply to library services management and includes guidance on the development of a QMS, including policies, processes, and procedures.

What Does an ISO 19814 Quality Management System Look Like?

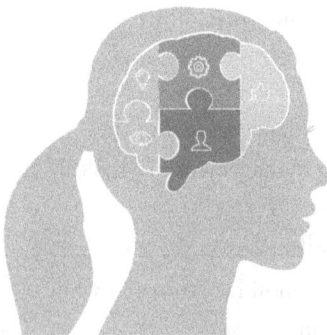

Quality Management
Comprises 5 basic factors including: Leadership; Planning; Resource Management; Service Delivery; and Measurement, Analysis, and Improvement

Leadership
- Clear, communicated vision
- Supported through regular analysis, testing, and verification

Planning
Measurable, clearly identified targets and objectives that align with organization's goals

Resource Management
Effectively managing resources including physical and digital collections, ensuring the availability of appropriate technology and equipment, budgeting, and policies and procedures

Service Delivery
Defining service standards, developing workflows and procedures for delivering services, and monitoring performance based on KPIs

Measurement, Analysis, and Improvement
- Collecting and analyzing data on library services, identifying areas for improvement, and implementing appropriate corrective actions
- Continuous improvement culture and developing processes for sharing best practices and lessons learned

---

[1] www.iso.org/standard/66263.html.

These elements include:

Leadership: Clearly communicated vision for the library's services and that they communicate that recommendation effectively to staff, stakeholders, and users that is supported by continuous improvement and provides the necessary resources and support to achieve this.

Planning: Measurable objectives and targets for their services, clearly identify the resources required to achieve these objectives, and develop policies and procedures that align with their vision and goals.

Resource management: Managing both physical and digital collections, ensuring the availability of appropriate technology and equipment, and developing policies and procedures for managing staff, finances, and other resources.

Service delivery: Defined service standards, developed workflows and procedures for delivering services, and monitoring performance against established objectives and targets.

Measurement, analysis, and improvement: Collecting and analyzing data on library services, identifying areas for improvement, and implementing appropriate corrective actions. Establishment of a continuous improvement culture and developing processes for sharing best practices and lessons learned.

Additional specific areas covered by ISO/TR 19814:2017 include the following.

Digital Resource Management

This includes the development of policies and procedures for the acquisition, management, and preservation of digital resources as well as processes for managing digital resources that meet the needs of library users and ensure resources are accessible and secure. Specific procedures in this area include:

Instituting policies and procedures governing how libraries should acquire digital resources, defining criteria for selecting those resources, negotiating licenses and access agreements, and establishing procedures for acquiring, cataloging, and processing digital resources

Establishing standards for long-term digital preservation and for the backup and migration of digital resources, and implementing the types of metadata standards that promote long-term accessibility (e.g., speed of access), quality, and usability of digital resources

Effectively managing digital rights, protecting the security and confidentiality of digital resources, and providing user support and training on their access and use

Defining staff workflows and roles, establishing appropriate technologies and infrastructure for digital resource management, and auditing and measuring performance based on clear KPIs

Continually evaluating resource impact and usage by collecting and analyzing relevant data, identifying usage trends, and applying this knowledge to inform decisions about resource allocation, acquisition, preservation, and access

Special Collection Management

ISO/TR 19814:2017 provides guidance on the management of special collections. Special collections are materials that are rare, unique, valuable, or fragile, and may include manuscripts, archives, rare books, photographs, maps, and other materials that require special care and handling. Specific standards include:

Creating a strategic plan that identifies the scope and nature of special collections; developing policies and procedures governing the acquisition of special collections materials; processing, preservation, and access; and establishing procedures for measuring and evaluating performance

Developing policies and procedures for acquiring and processing special collections that enable them to preserve and provide access to these materials; creating criteria for selecting materials to acquire; establishing procedures to assess condition; and developing defined mechanisms and procedures for the processing, cataloging, storage, and protection of materials within special collections

Enacting measures to ensure the long-term accessibility and usability of materials within special collections including developing a preservation plan to identify specific risks and threats; enacting environmental monitoring and related controls; developing policies to govern the handling and storing of special collection materials; and developing procedures for digitizing and providing access to materials

Ensuring access to special collections by establishing procedures for managing requests and providing access to materials; developing procedures for managing reproduction and publication requests; and providing user support and training

Monitoring special collections management by establishing performance metrics and targets, collecting and analyzing data on the use and impact of special collections, and using this information to inform decision making and improve performance

Interlibrary Loan Management

The ISO/TR 19814:2017 provides guidance on how libraries should manage interlibrary loan (ILL) services. The basis for this guidance is the recognition that ILL is an important service that allows libraries to provide access to materials that are not available in their own collections.

Important elements of this standard include the development of policies and procedures governing the provision and management of ILL services that facilitate the lending and borrowing of materials between libraries.

Specific elements include:

A recommendation that libraries develop policies and procedures for ILL that define the scope and nature of ILL services, establish criteria for eligible borrowers and lending libraries, and establish procedures for requesting and supplying materials

Procedures for managing ILL requests to verify borrower and library eligibility and to manage intellectual property rights compliance matters associated with ILL requests

Procedures for tracking and monitoring ILL requests that allow libraries to measure performance and identify areas for improvement by

instituting performance metrics and targets, collecting and analyzing ILL request data on ILL requests, and using this data effectively
to make informed lending decisions

Creating coherent mechanisms for managing ILL collections that
include storage and protection standards, standards for renewing
loans and for recalling materials loaned or borrowed through ILL
programs, and policies for managing lost or damaged materials

Creating methodologies to evaluate and audit ILL services including
performance metrics and targets and ILL impact data, and deploying this information to inform decision making and improve ILL
system performance.

By implementing the recommendations of ISO 19814:2017, libraries
can develop QMSs that are tailored to their specific needs and goals
and continuously improve their services based on performance metrics
and user feedback.

In one example, Library and Archives Canada (LAC) developed
a QMS that focused on improving the management of their digital
resources, which included policies and procedures for acquiring, preserving, and providing access to their digital collections and a system for monitoring the performance of their digital resource management processes.[2]

According to this plan, all relevant institutions should have a broad
internal policy in place to guide all digitization projects and programs.
This was backed by a series of fundamental policy principles regarding
digitized records including:

- *Usability*: A digitized record must be useable, have integrity,
  be deemed authentic and reliable, support all business
  activities, and be able to withstand legal scrutiny.
- *Uniformity*: A digitized record must be generated under
  set policies and practices, be fully documented, and be
  maintained within an official corporate repository.

---

[2] https://library-archives.canada.ca/eng/services/government-canada/information-
disposition/disposition-government-records/multi-institution-disposition-authori
zations/Pages/digitization-guidelines.aspx.

- *Authorized disposal*: Disposal of source analogue records may be carried out only by authorization of the Librarian and Archivist of Canada, for example, through an institution-specific Disposition Authorization or MIDA 2018/013 Disposition Authorization for the Destruction of Source Records following Digitization.
- *Stated purpose*: The policy should state the purpose of digitization, specify when digitization is appropriate, and set the institution's criteria for document selection. The policy should outline what criteria need to be set, approved, and documented for each digitization project.

In addition, a departmental procedures manual must be created and implemented to ensure that all digitization projects adhere to the same process and a comprehensive plan should be put in writing for each digitization project.[3]

In another example, the New York Public Library developed a QMS that included policies and procedures for managing the reference desk, providing research assistance, and collecting user feedback. The overall goal of the system was to increase the efficiency of the library's reference services and increase user satisfaction with the quality of their research assistance.[4]

---

[3] Id.
[4] www.nypl.org/node/5731.

CHAPTER 29

Developing Uniform Digitization Standards

Libraries, especially research libraries, are critical preservers and disseminators of important scientific, cultural, and historical materials, many of which are degradable or difficult to find and track when kept in physical format. Uniform digitization standards help libraries to ensure that these materials remain high quality and can be preserved and searched over time.

The main benefits of using uniform digitization standards include:

- Increased access to library collections.
- Improvement of interlibrary cooperation—digitization allows libraries and institutions to share data more easily and to track loaned materials.
- Efficiency—implementing uniform digitization standards can help libraries to streamline their digitization processes, scale their efforts, and lower digitization costs, by providing clear guidelines and best practices.

The summary of digitization standards that follows is based on a series of guidelines developed by Library Archives Canada. While there are others, we believe this standard to be a defensible and comprehensive general guideline for digitization best practices for research libraries.[1]

---

[1] https://library-archives.canada.ca/eng/services/government-canada/information-disposition/disposition-government-records/multi-institution-disposition-authorizations/Pages/digitization-guidelines.aspx.

Why Is Defensible Digitization Important?

Libraries and other similar institutions should digitize records in order to produce records that are authoritative, legally admissible as substitutes for the original source records, and accessible for as long as required. Instituting defensible, uniform standards allows institutions to ensure that their process of digitizing is documented, auditable, and reliable. Defensibility means that institutions should be able to demonstrate that a digitized record is a true and accurate version of the source record.

To demonstrate defensibility, institutions must demonstrate that they have engaged in planning, assessing, preparing, digitizing, and compiling metadata; running quality assurance checks; and storing and managing digitized records. And to be effective, these processes require institutions to institute and maintain policies and procedures governing their digitization processes, and to fully plan and document the digitization process.

One useful digitization-related standard is ISO/TR 21946:2018, which provides guidelines for organizations conducting appraisal for managing records, including in the digitization process.

This standard includes guidelines for:

- Identifying which records need to be appraised based on their business value, legal requirements, and other criteria
- Evaluating the value and significance of the identified records by measuring their administrative, legal, financial, historical, or research value
- Evaluating which retention and disposal schedules to use, reviewing those schedules when deciding on how long to keep records, and ensuring that the appraisal process manages records in accordance with applicable laws including privacy and retention laws
- Regularly consulting with stakeholders such as records creators, researchers, users, and managers to ensure that their priorities are heard when deciding which records to digitize
- Ensuring that the appraisal process is consistent with records management policies and procedures (and does not create unnecessary confusion)

ISO/TR 21946:2018 can be applied in the context of a library digitizing its collections by providing a framework for the appraisal of which digital records should be digitized for long-term preservation. The criteria in this standard can be used to identify the most important records for digitization; evaluate their value using accepted appraisal criteria; and develop, review, and apply retention and disposal schedules based on their significance and the applicable legal and institutional requirements.

Another useful framework, the National Data Stewardship Alliance (NDSA), provides a structured framework for assessing the strength of organizations' digital preservation levels and identifying problem areas and pain points.

These levels consist of four stages:

- Level 1 (Protect), which establishes basic policies and procedures for storage, backup, and security
- Level 2 (Store), which involves establishing more robust policies and procedures for storage and preservation of digital content
- Level 3 (Protect and Manage), which actively manages digital content over time to ensure its long-term accessibility and usability
- Level 4 (Mitigate), which involves actively mitigating risks to digital content by implementing advanced preservation strategies

Each of these levels builds on the strengths of the previous one, and organizations following the NDSA framework are, generally, encouraged to strive for higher levels of development as their capabilities mature. Libraries can use the NDSA levels to evaluate their current digital preservation practices and identify areas for improvement in these practices. For example, prior to digitizing records, it may be useful for a library to conduct a self-assessment of their digitization program against the NDSA levels and to develop a plan improvement and development of their internal digital content management standards. In addition, and perhaps more importantly, because the NDSA standards provide a common language, libraries can use the descriptions of NDSA levels to communicate the structure and timeline for their preservation practices to stakeholders and potential institutional and external funding sources, and as evidence of their commitment to best practices related to the long-term digital preservation of their collections.

When Should Digitization Planning Occur?

The scope of digitization activities will vary widely between institutions, ranging from occasional projects to formal digitization programs. Regardless, for digitization to be effective (and defensible), the institution must assess relevant considerations and priorities before commencing digitization work. This assessment is essential to ensure that every digitized record is authentic, is reliable, has integrity, and is usable. In addition, by adhering to a uniform set of guidelines, institutions can ensure that their digitized records will continue to meet their business requirements as the source records, both currently and in the future.

What Should a Digitization Policy Framework Look Like?

Prior to digitizing records, libraries and other institutions should establish a comprehensive internal policy to oversee their digitization projects and programs. This framework should be composed of the following fundamental principles:

- Digitized records must be usable; have integrity, authenticity, and reliability; support all business activities; and be legally defensible.
- Digitized records must be created under established policies and practices, fully documented, and maintained within an official corporate repository.
- Disposal of source analog records must be authorized by the relevant authority in charge of the institution.

In addition, the policy must clearly state the purpose of digitization, specify when digitization is appropriate, and define the institution's criteria for document selection and should delineate the criteria to be established, approved, and documented for each digitization project.

To ensure predictability, uniformity, scalability, and cost minimization, the institution should create a manual of departmental procedures to ensure that all digitization projects follow the same process. Where possible, a plan should also be developed for each digitization project (especially large-scale projects), outlining the digitization plan, project-specific benchmarks, and required approvals, and, in any event, all steps taken must be documented.

It is essential to distinguish between the policy, which will apply to all projects (i.e., the digitization program), and the specific project requirements. For instance, the policy must mandate that each digitization project must establish quality assurance criteria that are project specific, based on business needs, and recorded in a digitization manual.

Which Documents Should Be Digitized?

When deciding which records to digitize, it's important to consider user needs and document characteristics. Your institution's policy should include criteria for selecting suitable records for digitization.

Records that are frequently used, essential to services, needed for workflows, needed by multiple users, accessed remotely, difficult to access in their original format, or fragile and in need of protection during handling are all good candidates for digitization. However, some records may require more effort and cost to scan, such as those with unusual formats, those with multiple documents, or those that need special care.

On the other hand, transitory records, those with short retention periods, and those with intrinsic value or archival significance that should be kept in their original state and transferred to central archives should not be digitized unless confirmed by institutional archivists.

When Is It Appropriate to Use an Outsourced Digitization Solution?

When deciding whether to digitize in-house or outsource digitization work, an institution should consider various factors including whether the digitization will be a one-time project or an ongoing program.

Also, while outsourcing offers benefits such as lower upfront costs, budget control, economies of scale, and access to vendor expertise, it's essential to consider the security of records during transportation and digitization.

Moreover, institutions that use outsourced solutions must be able to ensure that they are able to constantly communicate with the vendor. And, finally, not all vendors are suitable. When choosing a suitable vendor, it is crucial to determine their ability to adhere to formal digitization or evidence standards, use appropriate technology, handle specific formats, and follow quality assurance practices, as well as their ability to provide a certification of assurance for all digitization activities.

Allocation of Roles and Responsibilities

Properly allocating roles and responsibilities (and adhering to them) is a critical success factor when seeking to ensure the success of a digitization project. It is particularly important for ensuring the authenticity and reliability of records and documenting approvals and accountability.

To increase the likelihood of a successful project outcome, a combination of skills from staff with different areas of expertise is required including legal, IT, finance, risk management, and other relevant departments, ideally, in the form of a steering committee. Clear roles and responsibilities, well-defined reporting lines, and detailed communication plans must be established.

It is also important to obtain a specific and formal authorization to destroy source records after digitization.

Risk Management

Prior to undertaking any digitization work, institutions should evaluate the potential risks associated with digitization (or not digitizing) of their records. The institution should document their tolerance for risk and outline any plans for mitigating such risks. The following are examples of risks:

- *Risk of destroying source records*: In some cases, the digitized version of a record may not be legally accepted as having evidentiary value. Institutions should consider factors such as whether it is feasible to digitize the record in a way that preserves its characteristics and meets legal requirements, whether the digitized image will meet quality standards, and the extent of loss or change in record characteristics that the institution is willing to accept.

- *Cost of digitization*: Institutions should compare the costs of digitizing versus maintaining the source records. It is also important to consider the cost of maintaining digital records over time as technology evolves and requires migration.
- *Risks involved in not digitizing*: Lack of efficiency in collaboration, high cost of long-term storage for analogue records, and deterioration of source records over time.

Institutions should carefully consider these risks and develop a plan for addressing them in order to ensure that their digitization projects are successful and that their records are preserved appropriately.

Format and Indexing

To ensure the appropriate format for digitized images, institutions should consider their business needs and legal requirements. For archival records, it is important to consult the parent institution's (or government entity's) official guidelines.

Notwithstanding, there are different types of digitization for paper records, each allowing for varying degrees of access: page images, full text, and encoded text. The format and access needed will determine the necessary indexing. For other formats, such as spatial information, institutions should determine the most appropriate digitization method.

Also, it is crucial for ensuring the accessibility, reliability, and proper management of digitized records. This process should occur at different stages of the digitization process and be retained for as long as the records themselves. Bibliographic indexing relates to the content and management of the record, while biographic indexing pertains to the digitization process and must be captured during scanning. Biographic metadata can include image reference, digitization date, equipment operator, and transfer details.

Preparation

To ensure high-quality digitized images, institutions must properly prepare the documents prior to digitizing. The amount of preparation required depends on the condition and format of the source records. Basic preparation is typically sufficient for efficient digitization, but folded, rolled, fragile, or damaged documents may require more extensive work. In cases where specialized equipment is needed, large format items may need to be scanned separately, and their original order should be documented in the metadata.

The personnel responsible for preparing the documents should identify any potential issues with them so that the scanner operator can make necessary adjustments.

Quality Assurance

The process of quality assurance involves verifying whether the digitized record satisfies the established requirements. It includes assessing the output and operation of digitization processes to ensure that the agreed-upon benchmarks have been met and that the digitized images are suitable replacements for the original record. The acceptability of the image quality is subjective and should be determined beforehand for each project, with the criteria documented. The required image quality is dependent on the purpose of the digitized record (e.g., whether it will serve as the official version of the record). It is recommended to scan to the highest possible quality to ensure authenticity.

For each digitization project or program, the institution should determine:

- The number of errors allowable in a sample.
- The sample size of the records to be examined.
- Who will perform the assessment?

In addition, to ensure defensibility, quality assurance activities should be recorded, and each batch of digitized images should be certified as having passed quality control. It is recommended that someone other than the equipment operator perform the quality assessment.

And, in addition, the quality control process should at a minimum:

- Verify image accuracy
- Ensure metadata quality and accuracy
- Confirm the completeness of the digitized version

Finally, it is important to classify errors as major or minor, including issues such as skewed images, insufficient contrast, illegible characters, and speckling on the image.

Quality control audits should be carried out at various stages throughout the digitization process, including image capture, recapture, indexing, quality assurance, and transfer of images. Finally, periodic quality control inspections should be conducted on all equipment used to ensure proper functioning and calibration.

CHAPTER 30

Classification and Integration of Digitized Records Into an Electronic Document and Records Management System (EDRMS)

The process of classification and integration into the electronic document and records management system (EDRMS) ensures that digitized images can be incorporated into the file classification system and the EDRMS. Digitized records must be assigned a file number and retention and disposition information, which should be aligned for analogue, digital, and digitized records. The content of a record, not its format, determines retention and disposition, sensitivity, and access permissions, and the digitized versions should have the same characteristics as the source records.

Derivative copies may be created with the official version of the record for various reasons. These copies should be identified as such in the file title by using naming conventions.

Security

Institutions should plan for both the physical security of the records and the security of the information during the digitization process. Protected and secret information should be added to the metadata of digitized records, and access restrictions should be applied to the digitized image as they were to the source record. If source records are being destroyed, they should be destroyed in a manner consistent with their security level.

Data Transfer

Departments or individual business units (such as libraries) must define procedures for the transfer of source documents and digitized files to ensure that records remain secure and that their authenticity has been maintained during transfer. Whatever method is used, it is important to ensure that the digitized files are not altered during transfer by using fixity information, such as a checksum.

Storage and Preservation

If active, records must be stored in a designated corporate repository that meets all requirements for the management of records throughout the full life cycle. If the digitized records are being put in dormant storage, the storage solution must have search and access capacity, can manage the records over long term, protect the authenticity of the record, and be responsive to regulatory and litigation requests. Departments or business units should plan for the necessary storage and a schedule for migration and/or conversion of digital records as technology changes.

Disposition of Source Records

In some instances, source records may be kept after digitization, but more frequently, they are destroyed. Institutional policy and procedures and evidence that they were followed are key to proving the authenticity of the records if their authenticity is challenged.

Documentation

A project manual should be created for each digitization initiative, which should include all the necessary information documented in one place, including specific choices made for metadata, quality control, and format.

CHAPTER 31

International Archival Standards

ISO 11799: 2015—Information and Documentation—Document Storage Requirements for Archive and Library Materials[1]

ISO 11799:2015 is an international standard that provides guidelines for document storage requirements for archive and library materials. It applies to the long-term storage of archive and library materials for their lifetime. It considers that the materials are stored and allow current usage as well.

Generally, the standard specifies the requirements for the storage of paper-based archival records, including documents, manuscripts, books, and maps. More specifically, the standard outlines the necessary conditions for storing archival materials, including temperature and humidity levels, lighting, and air quality. It also provides guidelines for the construction and maintenance of storage facilities, including requirements for fire suppression systems, pest control measures, and security systems. In addition, it provides recommendations for handling and transporting archival materials, including guidelines for packing and labeling materials for safe transport.

---

[1] www.iso.org/obp/ui/#iso:std:iso:11799:ed-2:v1:en.

At its core, the standard emphasizes the importance of monitoring and maintaining storage conditions to ensure the long-term preservation of archival materials. It recommends regular inspections and testing of storage environments to identify potential issues and ensure that conditions remain within acceptable ranges.

However, because national or local building regulations in different fields tend to cover topics such as construction, safety, and security for public buildings or those storing valuable objects, the standard avoids listing detailed rules and regulations in these areas, except for recommendations that may complement existing requirements.

Given is a summary of the specific recommendations of ISO 11799:2015.

Risk Management

Prior to determining how to store hard-copy archival records, libraries should conduct a comprehensive assessment, including a risk evaluation, to determine their need for and the potential risks associated with constructing an archive and/or library repository building.

The committee or individual charged with site selection for the archived area should consider various risks, such as flooding; subsidence or landslides; tsunamis; volcanic activity; earthquakes; adjacent site activities that may cause fires or explosions; accidents on nearby air runways or train tracks; proximity to strategic installations that may be a target during armed conflicts, terrorist attacks, or civil unrest; proximity to plants, installations, or natural sources that emit harmful gases, smoke, dust, and so on; and proximity to places or buildings that attract rodents, insects, and other pests.

In addition, the building design should be sufficiently stable so as to enable the library to mitigate hazards and protect the archived holdings against intentional harm, fire, water, pests, contaminants, light, UV, IR, temperature extremes or harmful fluctuations, and humidity extremes or harmful fluctuations. To minimize the harmful effects of external climatic variations, the building's orientation, landscaping, overall climate of the site, and construction should be carefully considered. Finally, the building should be designed to facilitate the safe movement of holdings and to assist recovery from significant threats by incorporating features such as smoke hatches, floor drains, and ramps.

Once constructed, the parties charged with formulating the design plan should conduct a postoccupancy evaluation to ensure that the objectives are met and the desired effects are achieved.

Regarding the construction of the building, the repository must be secured against theft, burglary, vandalism, and terrorism, and precautions should be taken against arson. In addition, ideally, the repository should be a purpose-built detached building or a self-contained unit within a building. And the building design should also facilitate monitoring and prevent unauthorized access through the entrances.

Finally, emergency exits shall be constructed in such a way that they can easily be opened from the inside and that they cannot be opened from the outside, with the exceptions for fire response. In the interests of security, it is recommended that storage areas should have no windows or skylight or they should be fitted to provide adequate security.

Internal Storage Environment

Maintaining a stable internal environment appropriate for preserving the holdings is crucial, and temperature and relative humidity greatly impact the materials. Therefore, storage areas should be designed to provide a stable internal environment that meets the preservation requirements of the materials.

Annex C of the standard specifies the requirements for the storage environment of archives and library materials. It provides specific guidelines for temperature, relative humidity, and air quality that should be maintained to preserve the materials. According to Annex C, the ideal temperature for storing paper-based materials is between 16°C and 19°C (60.8°F to 66.2°F), and the ideal relative humidity range is between 45 and 60 percent. However, these ranges may be adjusted based on the specific needs of the materials being stored. Annex C also recommends monitoring the storage environment using appropriate equipment, such as temperature and humidity sensors. Additionally, it suggests that storage areas should be regularly inspected for signs of mold, insects, and other pests.

One way to achieve a stable internal environment is to construct the external walls, roof, and floor of the building using materials that insulate the interior from external climatic changes, while still allowing for air supply and circulation required for both collection storage and human occupancy. The walls, floors, and ceilings inside the repository should be made of materials with high thermal inertia and moisture-buffering capacity.

In addition, the standard recommends maintaining positive or neutral air pressure in repositories so that the library can maintain an appropriate conditioned environment and prevent dust, pollutants, and unconditioned air from entering the room.

Inner Structure and Load Requirements

To enable libraries to maintain efficient climate control, fire safety, and minimal loss of holdings in the event of a fire, the standard recommends compartmentalizing the repository. On a practical level, this means that walls (including doors), floors, and ceilings between single rooms and compartments, and between storage and other areas of the building, should be constructed in a manner that prevents fire (and water) from spreading into a neighboring unit. Additionally, the floor load must be calculated considering the specific volume and type(s) of archival records, the containers, and the static or movable shelving, cabinets, and/or cases. And structural support overall, or in specific higher load areas, should be maintained.

During design, it is recommended for libraries to consider installing a shelving configuration that ensures appropriate structural support, aisle width, and movement of materials for the types of materials and containers to be stored. Drains are recommended if water is used for fire protection, with protection against the entry of pests and water. Drainage should be configured to carry water completely away from the building.

Finally, in order to enable safe and efficient movement of holdings, space should be provided for inner structural supports and doorways. All inner structural systems should be engineered with bracing to resist movement or tipping that could result in a collapse or other damage to the holdings.

Fire Prevention

Annex A of the standard recommends that libraries should implement fire prevention and protection measures in the design of the building and storage areas and should also list these measures within their policies and procedures for the management of archival holdings.

Importantly, Annex A recommends that the repository should be designed to minimize the risk of fire, with proper separation of areas to prevent the spread of fire and adequate ventilation to prevent the accumulation of combustible gases. The use of flammable materials in the construction of the repository should be avoided, and the repository should be equipped with an appropriate fire detection and alarm system.

In addition, appropriate fire suppression systems should be installed, such as sprinkler systems, and fire drills and training should be conducted regularly. Finally, libraries should take a proactive approach that ensures fire safety is accounted for when selecting materials for storage and that all materials should be stored in a manner that minimizes the risk of combustion or ignition.

With respect to fire detection, the standard recommends that libraries install a fire detection system that connects to a central monitoring panel in all areas of the building. This system should automatically detect smoke or other combustion products, and heat detection devices should only be used in areas where other types of detectors may not be suitable.

Additionally, manually operated fire-alarm call points should be provided throughout the building for use by occupants in the event of a fire. The central fire-alarm control panel should allow for monitoring of all components of the system and provide a visual display of the system status. The panel should be located in a central, convenient location that is continuously monitored while the repository is occupied or open. If the panel is not located at or near the likely fire-brigade entry point, a supplementary or repeater panel should be installed for the use of the fire brigade.

Fire extinguishers should be provided in the repository, and the benefits of an automatic firefighting system should be considered. Gas or water-based firefighting systems with no additives are recommended for repositories. Fire extinguishing measures should be designed with consideration for the materials stored, building design, size of fire compartments, higher-density structure, type of shelving, and other relevant factors.

Illumination/Light

Given the sensitivity of many of the materials stored in hard-archival format, it is critical for libraries to avoid the impact of the harmful effects of light on materials stored in the repository by controlling the intensity, duration, and spectral distribution of illumination.

In particular, libraries should take measures to exclude direct daylight, and windows should be blocked or screened by curtains or blinds. These precautions are also recommended for offices, public reading rooms, and other rooms where documents are exhibited. Illumination should be kept to a minimum and powered off when not needed through time controls, motion detection, or other means. According to the standard, a maximum illumination level of 100 lux on the floor level is sufficient for retrieval, replacement, room inspection, and cleaning. The distance between the lamp and unprotected materials should be considered in relation to the heat the lamp generates.

Humidity

Another potentially serious danger to archival materials is humidity. The standard recommends that repositories for archive and library materials should be kept at a relative humidity below the point where microbiological activity occurs and at a cool temperature, ideally in a building with high thermal and hydric inertia. Different materials have different recommended limits for temperature and humidity, and there is no general agreement. The specific criteria for humidity are outlined in Annex C, as discussed earlier.

Ventilation

Maintaining continual air ventilation is necessary for libraries seeking to keep records clean and dry, as well as to discourage microorganisms and prevent mold outbreaks. The standard recommends that air exchanges and circulation are necessary to minimize the risk of developing microclimates that may cause mold growth and prevent the buildup of off-gassing from the holdings.

Libraries that fail to maintain proper ventilation standards are likely to experience a growth of microorganisms, and, as a result, a particulate filtration system should be designed for both air supply and return air ducting if necessary. To avoid exposure to an internal source of particulates, concrete block walls should be primed and painted, and concrete floors should be hardened with sealant.

Gaseous Contaminants

The standard notes that gaseous contaminants can cause irreversible damage to holdings and that this damage is both cumulative and heavily influenced by other environmental factors such as relative humidity and temperature.

Annex D provides information on gaseous pollutants and their effects on library and archive materials and provides a number of suggestions as to how libraries can avoid gaseous contaminant exposure.

These measures include:

- Identifying potential sources of gaseous pollutants in the document repository area and taking specific steps to minimize their emissions
- Maintaining temperature and relative humidity levels that are appropriate for the materials being stored (as discussed in Annex C)
- Regularly monitoring the concentration of gaseous pollutants and taking necessary corrective action
- Considering the use of activated carbon or other air-cleaning systems to remove gaseous pollutants
- Encouraging the use of materials that are less prone to off-gassing, such as stainless steel or inert plastics, for storage cabinets, shelves, and other furniture

- Storing materials in acid-free enclosures or containers to minimize exposure to gaseous pollutants
- Conducting regular inspections of the repository area to detect signs of deterioration or damage caused by gaseous pollutants

Overall, the standard, together with its annexes, seeks to provide libraries with a series of concrete guidelines to ensure that their hard-copy archival and library materials are preserved in a suitable environment that will minimize the risk of damage or loss.

The Importance of Using Proper Archival Descriptions

One of the most important tasks of the modern digital librarian is to manage and maintain archives. To accomplish this task properly, it is important to use uniform and generally accepted archival principles.

The purpose of the archival description is to identify and explain the context and content of archival material in order to promote its accessibility.[2]

This is achieved by creating accurate and appropriate representations and by organizing them in accordance with predetermined models.

Description-related processes may begin at or before records creation and continue throughout the life of the records. These processes make it possible to institute the intellectual controls necessary for reliable, authentic, meaningful, and accessible descriptive records to be carried forward through time.

During the archival process, specific elements of information about archival materials must be recorded at every phase of data management (e.g., creation, appraisal, accessioning, conservation, and arrangement). This is important for both the secure preservation and control of relevant records and for the organization's needs to access them and provide them to the public. In addition, using proper archival descriptions ensures that relevant records can be properly updated, which is particularly important for data that is stored in computerized record repositories. And these processes are relevant, not only for data that has been selected

---

[2] ISAD(G) 2nd. edition (ica.org).

for preservation, but also in the preselection phase, where librarians and related professionals are choosing which documents are worthy of preservation within the institution's system.

On a practical level, using official, established, and general rules for archival description helps organizations to:

- Ensure the creation of consistent, appropriate, and self-explanatory descriptions.
- Facilitate the retrieval and exchange of information about archival material.
- Enable the sharing of authority data.
- Make possible the integration of descriptions from different locations into a unified information system.

The ISAD(G): General International Standard Archival Description adopted by the Committee on Descriptive Standards in Stockholm, Sweden, organizes these rules into seven distinct information management standards:

1. Identity Statement Area (where essential information is conveyed to identify the unit of description)
2. Context Area (where information is conveyed about the origin and custody of the unit of description)
3. Content and Structure Area (where information is conveyed about the subject matter and arrangement of the unit of description)
4. Condition of Access and Use Area (where information is conveyed about the availability of the unit of description)
5. Allied Materials Area (where information is conveyed about materials having an important relationship to the unit of description)
6. Note Area (where specialized information and information that cannot be accommodated in any of the other areas may be conveyed)
7. Description Control Area (where information is conveyed on how, when, and by whom the archival description was prepared)

The ISAD(G) standard also identifies a further 26 elements covered by these general rules. The most important of these elements, particularly in the context of the international exchange of descriptive information, are:

a. Reference code
b. Title
c. Creator
d. Date(s)
e. Extent of the unit of description
f. Level of description

In addition to this framework, ISO 28560-1:2011 specifies a standard data model and encoding formats for data elements used in the RFID tagging of library items. The goal of this standard is to facilitate interoperability between library systems and to enable consistent use of RFID technology across different libraries and regions, and its core requirements include:

- Adoption of a standard data model for the RFID tagging of library items, which includes data elements such as item identifier, bibliographic information, and circulation status
- Encoding formats for each data element, including character sets, data types, and data lengths
- The institution of guidelines mandating the use of certain data elements, such as how to encode a unique item identifier and how to indicate the type of material being tagged
- Rules for the placement of RFID tags on library items, including requirements for tag orientation and distance from the spine
- Guidelines for the use of RFID technology in circulation workflows, such as how to read and write RFID tags and how to handle privacy and security concerns

ISO 13008:2022—Information and Documentation— Digital Records Conversion and Migration Process

ISO 13008:2022 provides guidance for the conversion of records from one format to another and the migration of records from one hardware or software configuration to another. It contains applicable records management requirements, the organizational and business framework for conducting the conversion and migration process, technology planning issues, and monitoring/controls for the process. It also identifies the steps, components, and particular methodologies for each of these processes, covering such topics as workflow, testing, version control, and validation.

Conversion and migration are two common methods used in digital preservation that can impact an organization's overall preservation strategy. Libraries recognize the value of standardized procedures and have established test beds and task forces to explore and research different preservation methods, including conversion, migration, emulation, and refreshment, to determine the most effective approach for their needs.

To ensure the authenticity, reliability, integrity, and usability of digital records, it is essential to manage the conversion and migration processes effectively. ISO 13008:2022 outlines the program components, planning issues, and records management requirements for performing digital record conversion and migration. The document emphasizes the importance of preserving record integrity and adherence to relevant legal and regulatory requirements.

Organizations should be aware of the records management requirements before beginning a conversion or migration project, and individuals designated as key to the process should be knowledgeable about these requirements. The principles of record integrity, authenticity, reliability, and usability apply to both ad hoc and ongoing conversion or migration programs. Future planning for further conversion and migration of records should be incorporated into requirements for electronic document and records management systems (EDRMS) to ensure long-term preservation of digital records.

Key elements of this standard as they apply to libraries include:

- *Scope and purpose*: The standard provides guidelines for the conversion and migration of digital records, including metadata and associated contextual information, to ensure the long-term preservation and accessibility of these records.
- *Principles*: The standard emphasizes the importance of maintaining the authenticity, integrity, reliability, and

usability of digital records throughout the conversion and migration process. It also stresses the need for appropriate documentation and communication throughout the process.

- *Planning and scoping*: The standard recommends that organizations develop a comprehensive plan for the conversion and migration process, including the identification of risks, stakeholders, and resources. It also emphasizes the importance of scoping the project appropriately to ensure its success.

- *Selection and evaluation of conversion and migration tools*: The standard recommends that organizations carefully evaluate and select the tools and methods used for the conversion and migration of digital records, based on factors such as their suitability, reliability, and compatibility with existing systems.

- *Metadata*: The standard emphasizes the importance of preserving and migrating metadata along with digital records, to ensure their continued accessibility and usability.

- *Quality control*: The standard recommends that organizations implement quality control measures throughout the conversion and migration process, including regular testing and evaluation, to ensure that the integrity and authenticity of digital records are maintained.

- *Documentation and reporting*: The standard recommends that organizations maintain appropriate documentation and reporting throughout the conversion and migration process, to enable future access and understanding of the records and their history.

One government standard that is based on ISO 13008, published by the provincial government of Alberta, Canada,[3] requires the following activities to be completed for a successful digital conversion or migration process, to ensure that recordkeeping is met.

---

[3] https://imtpolicy.sp.alberta.ca/standards/pdf/Digital-Records-Conversion-Migration-Standard_V1.1.pdf.

Based on this standard, for libraries undertaking information governance implementation projects, the following points are applicable for digital records conversion and migration:

- Perform all conversion and migration process testing on a sample copy of the records to identify and correct problems before irreversible activities are undertaken.
- Ensure that the originating file is not deleted until the conversion or migration result is verified and all jurisdictional legislative and policy requirements are met.
- Establish a methodology for comparing the content, context, and structure of the converted/migrated records with those of the source records to identify and correct problems and validate the conversion/migration result. The source records may be disposed of once the validation is complete, and all problems are fixed, and such decisions are documented and validated.
- Document all conversion and migration activities to demonstrate that all records, including those created while the conversion/migration activities were in progress, have been converted or migrated and are complete, accessible, and authentic throughout their full retention period.
- Ensure that the processes applied to the new format yield consistent results compared to the same or similar processes applied in the originating format.
- Document any damage or loss of digital information that may occur before the conversion or migration and aim to reduce the risk of further degradation of the content, context, and structure of the records to an absolute minimum.
- Consider physical and logical security during the conversion or migration, including access control to IT suites and the platform, without affecting existing access rights to the data.
- Define the metadata and data needed to retain the ability to reproduce a complete and authentic record, protect this data during the conversion or migration, and define the metadata

needed to identify and use the record for search and access after the conversion or migration.

- Document any attributes of the record that should not be converted or migrated to the new format or system and state the reason.
- Identify and establish safeguards to protect relational or linked records and relationships that could be compromised by the conversion or migration.
- Determine whether the appearance of the record contributes to its meaning as a digital record and address how to maintain it if appearance is integral to the meaning. Document any changes to the appearance of the record after the conversion or migration is complete.
- Define the targeted format of the records and aim to convert or migrate them as quickly as possible before the current format becomes obsolete.
- Evaluate the extent of the process metadata and decide whether some or all of this metadata should be converted or migrated.
- Create event history metadata for every individual record converted or migrated during the conversion or migration process to ensure the ability to make assertions on the authenticity of the record.
- Maintain relationships documented in metadata during the conversion or migration process, including internal, functional, aggregational, structural, and systematic relationships between records and control tools.

Libraries can use this standard to guide the implementation of digital recordkeeping systems and the conversion or migration of existing digital records. Given are a few use cases for libraries:

- *Migration of legacy digital records*: Libraries may have a large collection of digital records that were created using obsolete technology, such as floppy disks or old software programs. This standard can be used to guide the migration of these records to a more modern, sustainable format that meets current recordkeeping requirements.

- *Implementation of new digital recordkeeping systems*: Libraries may be implementing new digital recordkeeping systems, such as electronic resource management systems or digital archives. This standard can help ensure that the new systems are implemented in a way that preserves the authenticity and reliability of the records.
- *Preservation of born-digital records*: Libraries may be acquiring born-digital records, such as e-mail correspondence, social media content, or digital photographs. This standard can guide the implementation of preservation strategies that ensure the long-term viability of these records.

ISO/TR 13028:2012—Information and Documentation—Implementation Guidelines for Digitization of Records

At the outset, this standard outlines a series of potential benefits and risks related to digitization. These benefits and risks apply in a variety of business situations including in libraries undergoing digital transformation processes. Specific benefits include:

- Increased capacity for multiple users to access digital images simultaneously.
- Networked access allowing access to the images from multiple locations at any time.
- Greater integration with business information systems, providing greater efficiency and reducing manual data entry.
- Structured workflows can be implemented to help with processing and transmitting images.
- Hybrid systems can be eliminated, reducing confusion for users requiring access to the whole history of a matter.
- Resources that were limited in their reuse by their format can be reused.

- Consistent classification and indexing can be applied for better document retrieval, particularly for hybrid files.
- Integration with existing organizational disaster recovery and backup systems, ensuring business continuity.
- Provision of a protected and secured rendition, ensuring the security and integrity of the information.
- Reduced physical storage space required for hard-copy records, freeing up valuable space and reducing costs.
- Increased organizational productivity, reducing manual processes and allowing for more efficient workflows.

However, there are also risks associated with the digitization process, including:

- Short-term cost savings in space may be negated by longer-term costs associated with maintaining the accessibility of digital images over time.
- Technology and technical standards used to create digital images may significantly affect longevity and capacity to reuse the images in the future.
- Legislative, regulatory, or other requirements may limit the capacity to deploy commonly offered digitization features, such as image manipulation, if they do not maintain authentic and reliable representations of nondigital source records.
- It may not be appropriate to destroy the nondigital source records after the digitization process, especially where there are good reasons to retain the records in their nondigital form.
- Some specific classes of records have to be retained in their original format by law, and in some instances nondigitized records may need to be retained along with their digitized counterparts for a period of time.

To mitigate these risks, libraries undergoing digital transformation processes should carefully consider their digitization strategy and ensure compliance with all relevant legislative, regulatory, and information governance requirements. This may include implementing processes to ensure the long-term preservation of digital records, as well as developing policies and procedures to ensure the authenticity and reliability of digital images. Additionally, staff training and education may be necessary to ensure that all stakeholders are aware of the benefits and risks associated with digitization and are equipped to manage these risks effectively.

In the context of libraries undergoing digital transformation, the concept of master copies and derivative versions applies to the management of digitized records. Master copies refer to the original digital files that are kept in a secure storage environment and are used to produce derivative copies for access and use by library patrons. Derivatives are copies that are created during the digitization process, often in different formats or resolutions to accommodate different uses.

It is important for libraries to consider the legislative framework in which they operate when deciding whether to create master and derivative copies. In some cases, a master copy may not be necessary for records that are used for business decisions or as supporting reference material. However, for records that serve as evidence of a business action, a master copy may be required to ensure ongoing evidence of that activity.

Before destroying any master or derivative copies, libraries should conduct analyses of their business processes and identify the appropriate format of the record that is needed to manage the ongoing evidence of the business activity, according to any jurisdictional records legislation or regulatory requirements. This analysis ensures that the appropriate version of the record is retained for compliance purposes and that the organization is able to effectively manage and provide access to its digital records.

For libraries undergoing digital transformation, it is important to plan, scope, and document all digitization and digitization processes. The project documentation should include clear identification of business drivers, objectives, and constraints, as well as a statement of the purpose and expected uses of the digitized records. Additionally, the documentation should identify the benefits anticipated from the digitization and the impacts on users, as well as the technical standards adopted, equipment and resources needed, and processes for planning, control, and execution. Quality control processes should also be established, along with strategies for integrating the digitized image into work processes to support business actions. Ongoing management of the digitized records and non-digital source records should also be considered, along with legal requirements for digitization of record types.

The following basic criteria should be adhered to when selecting technical standards:

- The highest quality technical specifications that can be realistically supported should be incorporated into the digitization process.
- The formats should be open source (i.e., nonproprietary) or employ open standards, have published technical specifications available in the public domain, or be widely deployed within the relevant sector.
- The formats should not contain embedded objects, or link out to external objects beyond the specific version of the format.
- The formats should be supported by many software applications and operating systems.
- The formats should be able to be read by utilizing a readily available viewing plug-in if the specific production software is not available to all users.
- A body of accessible and product-independent technical expertise should be available to support the decision.
- Adequate technical support should exist to enable ongoing maintenance and migration capability when necessary.
- The master copies should be created to the highest technical standards that can be supported.
- The derivative copies may be made in formats most convenient for their business purpose (e.g., thumbnails for distribution over the Internet).

Clause 6 of this standard establishes a series of best practices for digitizing records. Given is a summary of how these practices apply in the concept of libraries undergoing digital transformation processes:

- *Planning*: This involves setting objectives and identifying the scope of the digitization project. The plan should also identify the resources required, risks associated with the project, and the timelines for the project. All digitization and digitization processes should be planned, scoped, and documented. The project documentation should include:

- o A scope definition, with clear identification of business drivers, objectives, scale, size, and constraints of the project.
- o A statement of the purpose and expected uses of the digitized records, illustrated if necessary with examples.
- o A statement of benefits: clear identification of the benefits anticipated from the digitization.
- o A statement of user needs and impacts: for example, how the digitized records are to be used and accessed and how this impacts users.
- o A statement of technical standards adopted: including format, compression, and metadata.
- o Equipment and resources to support the digitization.
- o Processes for the planning, control, and execution of the digitization, including those undertaken prior to, during, and after digitization.
- o Quality control processes.
- o Strategies for integrating the digitized image into work processes to support the business action taking place.
- o Strategies for the ongoing management of the digitized records and nondigital source records for as long as they are required to be maintained.
- o Strategies regarding the legal requirements for digitization of the record types in question.
- *Selection of materials*: Libraries need to determine which materials to digitize based on their value, condition, and copyright status. This selection process should be guided by a clear policy and criteria for selecting materials for digitization. In addition:
  - o The digitization approach selected should be documented.
  - o Quality control processes should be implemented regardless of the digitization approach adopted.

- o The digitization approach should be regularly reviewed for continuing compliance with the requirements of the legal environment, relevance, and cost effectiveness.
- *Preparing materials for digitization*: This involves preparing the physical materials for digitization, including cleaning, repairing, and assessing their condition. It also involves creating metadata and describing the materials to make them easily discoverable.
- *Digitization*: This involves the actual conversion of physical materials into digital form. Libraries should follow industry best practices and use high-quality scanners or cameras to ensure accurate and high-resolution images. They should also ensure that the digitization process does not damage the original materials.
- *Quality control*: Libraries should establish quality control procedures to ensure that the digital images are of sufficient quality and accuracy. This involves verifying that the images meet the required standards and are free from errors and inconsistencies.
- *Preservation*: Libraries should ensure that the digital materials are preserved for the long term. This involves selecting appropriate file formats, establishing backup and disaster recovery procedures, and creating multiple copies of the digital files.
- *Access and dissemination*: Libraries should make the digital materials accessible to users through appropriate channels, such as online platforms or physical media. They should also establish policies and procedures for sharing the digital materials while ensuring that copyright laws are respected.

Given next are fact patterns illustrating best-practice compliance for library digitization projects:

A library is digitizing a collection of rare manuscripts. They follow best practices for preparing the materials for digitization, including repairing damaged pages and creating detailed metadata. They use high-quality scanners to create accurate digital images and establish quality control procedures to ensure that the images are of sufficient quality. They select appropriate file formats and establish backup procedures to ensure the long-term preservation of the digital materials. Finally, they make the digital materials available to researchers through an online platform.

A library is digitizing a collection of photographs from a local historical society. They follow best practices for selecting materials for digitization, including obtaining permission from the copyright holder to digitize the materials. They use high-quality cameras to create digital images and establish quality control procedures to ensure that the images are free from errors and inconsistencies. They select appropriate file formats and establish backup and disaster recovery procedures to ensure the long-term preservation of the digital materials. Finally, they make the digital materials accessible to the public through a physical exhibit and an online platform.

ISO TC46/SC11—Archives/Records Management[4]

ISO TC46/SC11 was instituted in 1998 to reflect the growing need for standardization, on an international level, within records and archives management and the need to create common understanding at this moment of recordkeeping by including and synthesizing developments in different initiatives around the world.[5]

Core elements of this standard include:

- Rules for maintaining metadata
- Standards for digital repositories and preservation of digital records
- Records on the Web
- Management and business perspectives
- e-Government

---

[4] ISO – ISO/TC 46/SC 11 – Archives/records management.
[5] Microsoft Word – DLM Forum 2005_paper_Hofman.doc (interpares.org); the results of projects such as Inter Pares, the Australian RKMS project, or the Clever Metadata project of Monash University in Melbourne, for example, feed into the ISO work.

- e-Business
- Data as records—or records as data[6]

This standard also reflected the growing need for globalization—common standards are necessary if we are to be able to communicate and understand other people and organizations to trust, manage, and maintain messages and other important information. Good recordkeeping is an essential part of this process.[7]

ISO/TC 46/SC11 published three pieces of work related to metadata for records. These are known as the ISO 23081 series[8]:

- ISO 23081-1 Information and documentation—Records management processes—Metadata for records—Part 1: Principles sets forth a principles-based standard which links requirements for metadata to the core professional statements in the foundational ISO 15489-1.
- ISO 23081-2:2009 Information and documentation— Managing metadata for records—Part 2: Conceptual and implementation issues describes a practical approach to implementation, providing discussion on implementation options, managing metadata and a conceptual model for defining metadata elements for records.
- ISO/TR 23081-3:2011 Information and documentation— Managing metadata for records—Part 3: Self provides a self-assessment checklist in excel format to allow implementers to assess the strengths and weaknesses of their metadata schema against the requirements of the standard.

The central purpose of these standards is to define the metadata needed to show that an electronic object has been managed as a record over all the events that may take place during its physical existence, that

---

[6] Microsoft PowerPoint – Presentation 2 – Relationships – SC11 & IT21 – David Moldrich V2 (standards.org.au).

[7] Id.

[8] ISO 23081 Metadata for records.

is, the digital object can be interpreted in the context of the business and people that do the business and that support assertions about the characteristics of integrity, authenticity, reliability, and usability. It provides critical guidance for designing technical specifications for records that will be applied in specific technological applications and can be used to support assertions of authenticity and reliability at a point in time, and in all business and records environments.[9]

Additional sources related to metadata include:

- ISO 2709 "Format for information exchange," which specifies an exchange format for bibliographic metadata produced by libraries. It is supported by most libraries which produce a machine-readable catalogue.
- ISO 23950 "Information retrieval standard," which enables the seamless integration of searching between bibliographic databases. Most widely used integrated library systems support the standard, which makes it possible to copy catalogued bibliographic records between libraries.[10]

---

[9] Id.

[10] ISO_TC_046__Information_and_documentation_.pdf.

CHAPTER 32

ISO Standards for Recordkeeping

Why Are International Standards Important?[1]

In the area of information governance (IG), international standards serve a number of mission-critical goals, which closely align with the general goals of IG. These include:

- Establishing baseline criteria for creating, modifying, and maintaining data.
- Streamlining internal processes and embedding effectiveness and efficiency, particularly with respect to avoiding repeat work and allowing entities to create a clear data trail showing prior efforts and research.
- Reducing costs including, without limitation, storage costs and litigation discovery or regulatory reply costs.
- Improving business outcomes, by assisting organizations to measure performance through tracked data.
- Compliance—numerous laws and regulations such as (without limitation) retention standards and privacy laws dictate how organizations must keep and dispose of information.
- Risk mitigation.

---

[1] Microsoft PowerPoint – Presentation 2 – Relationships – SC11 & IT21 – David Moldrich V2 (standards.org.au).

As of the current date, the ISO Committee has published 19 standards:[2]

- ISO 13008:2012—Information and documentation—Digital records conversion and migration process
- ISO/TR 13028:2010—Information and documentation—Implementation guidelines for digitization of records
- ISO 15489-1:2016—Information and documentation—Records management—Part 1: Concepts and principles
- ISO 16175-1:2020—Information and documentation—Processes and functional requirements for software for managing records—Part 1: Functional requirements and associated guidance for any applications that manage digital records
- ISO/TS 16175-2:2020—Information and documentation—Processes and functional requirements for software for managing records—Part 2: Guidance for selecting, designing, implementing and maintaining software for managing records
- ISO 17068—Information and documentation—Trusted third party repository for digital records
- ISO/TR 18128:2014—Information and documentation—Risk assessment for records processes and systems
- ISO/TR 21946:2018—Information and documentation—Appraisal for managing records
- ISO/TR 21965:2019—Information and documentation—Records management in enterprise architecture
- ISO 22310:2006—Information and documentation—Guidelines for standards drafters for stating records management requirements in standards
- ISO/TR 22428-1:2020—Managing records in cloud computing environments—Part 1: Issues and concerns
- ISO 23081-1—Information and documentation—Records management processes—Metadata for records—Part 1: Principles

---

[2] ISO – ISO/TC 46/SC 11 – Archives/records management.

- ISO 23081-2:2021—Information and documentation—Metadata for managing records—Part 2: Conceptual and implementation issues
- ISO/TR 23081-3:2011—Information and documentation—Managing metadata for records—Part 3: Self-assessment method
- ISO/TR 26122:2008—Information and documentation—Work process analysis for records
- ISO/TR 26122:2008/COR 1:2009—Information and documentation—Work process analysis for records—Technical Corrigendum 1
- ISO 30300:2020—Information and documentation—Records management—Core concepts and vocabulary
- ISO 30301:2019—Information and documentation—Management systems for records—Requirements
- ISO 30302:2022—Information and documentation—Management systems for records—Guidelines for implementation

From a library science perspective, one of the most important elements addressed by the ISO is metadata. Using uniform standards for metadata (or, data about data) is critical to the librarian's task of ensuring that the right documents or records can be found at the right time. It is an inseparable part of records management, serving a variety of functions and purposes. In a records management context, metadata are defined as data describing the context, content, and structure of records and their management through time (ISO 15489-1:2001, 3.12).

Also, the effective use of metadata enables the creation, registration, classification, access, preservation, and disposition of records through time and within and across platforms. Another important reason to effectively manage metadata is that its management is closely related to the necessity by all organizations to avoid duplicative work—recreating metadata every time that documents or records are received by another organization is ineffective, is costly, and can lead to error.[3]

---

[3] Microsoft Word – DLM Forum 2005_paper_Hofman.doc (interpares.org).

ISO 15489:2016—Records Management (and Related Standards)

ISO 15489 Records Management, the first global standard for records management, was published in 2001, following which it was adopted in more than 50 countries and translated to over 15 languages. Thereafter, following a three-year period of review and consultation, a revised version of ISO 15489 Part 1 was issued in 2016.[4]

ISO considers records as evidence of business activity and valuable information assets, with varying degrees of reliance depending on the type of business. The standard provides guidelines for creating a records management policy that outlines an organization's approach to managing records, ensuring compliance with local regulations while meeting world-class standards. The first part of the standard, in particular, highlights the principles and concepts of a records management approach, helping organizations establish responsibilities, procedures, access, security, and monitoring for their records. In addition, it is important to note that ISO 15489 applies to records regardless of structure or form, in all types of business and technological environments, and over time.

Core principles of the standard include:

- Broad applicability not only to records, but to records systems and metadata for records
- Stated policies, assigned responsibilities, monitoring, and training supporting the effective management of records
- Recurring analysis of business context and the identification of records requirements
- The requirement to institute records controls
- The obligation to institute and maintain processes for creating, capturing, and managing records[5]

Main obligations include:

---

[4] ISO 15489 Records management.
[5] Id.

Leadership

- Organizations must establish a records management policy that includes, at least, a description of the purpose, scope, responsibilities, legal and regulatory requirements, as well as standards and best practices, procedures, access and security, training and awareness, monitoring and review, and records retention.
- Assign responsibilities for records management, including, for example, identifying the individuals or roles within an organization that are responsible for managing different aspects of the records management process, such as a steering committee, and assigning responsibility for creating, classifying, storing, maintaining, and disposing of records.
- Ensure that the necessary resources are available for records management, including identifying and allocating the necessary resources to maintain a records management program and auditing resource use.
- Communicate the importance of records management to the organization.

Planning

- Develop a records management plan that includes the scope and objectives of the program.[6]
- Identify the records that need to be managed.
- Develop ISO-compliant procedures for the creation, capture, and management of records—in particular, using metadata (or data about data), which ISO 15489 views as integral to records management, and which must be complete and

---

[6] An example of scope is a general statement that the plan covers all records created, received, and maintained by the organization in all formats and media, including paper and electronic records. The plan will apply to all functional areas and departments within the organization, and all staff members will be responsible for complying with the plan's requirements. Examples of objectives include compliance, efficiency, access, preservation, and security (described in detail).

accurate at the time of creation, so as to allow records to be managed effectively.[7]

- Develop defensible, relevant, and up-to-date retention and disposition schedules for records.[8]
- Develop procedures for the protection and preservation of records including security procedures such as physical and environmental protections, security policies, temperature controls and archiving procedures, software licenses, and information security procedures such as encryption, Virtual Private Networks (VPNs),[9] and access controls.
- Develop ISO-compliant procedures for the migration, conversion, and disposal of records.

Support

- Provide the necessary resources for records management, including personnel, technology, and infrastructure.
- Develop and deliver suitable training programs for records management.
- Provide guidance and assistance to staff on records management issues, including policies and procedures.
- Ensure that records management is integrated into the organization's processes and systems (e.g., IG by design).

---

[7] ISO 15489 provides specific guidelines for managing metadata in records management, including capturing complete and accurate metadata at record creation, managing metadata throughout the record's life cycle, identifying types of metadata, managing metadata as a record, ensuring its accuracy and accessibility, securing metadata, and documenting metadata management procedures.

[8] Under ISO 15489, a defensible retention and disposition schedule should identify the types of records to be retained, specify the length of time that each type of record will be kept, ensure compliance with legal and regulatory requirements, and include procedures for the disposition of records at the end of their retention period. Also, the schedule should be regularly reviewed and updated to reflect changes in the organization's business activities or legal and regulatory requirements.

[9] Virtual Private Network or VPN is the use of a secure, apparently private network that encrypts data over a public network.

Operation

- Create and capture records in a systematic and consistent manner in compliance with ISO standards.
- Classify and index records in a way that enables easy retrieval and use, so as to enable searchability.
- Ensure the integrity and authenticity of records, so that stakeholders can rely on the "right" versions.
- Manage access to records in accordance with the organization's policies and procedures.
- Manage the storage and retrieval of records.
- Ensure that records are disposed of in a timely and appropriate manner.

Performance Evaluation

- Monitor and measure the performance of the records management program.
- Conduct internal audits of the program.
- Identify areas for improvement in the program.
- Report on the performance of the program to management.

Improvement

- Identify opportunities for improvement in the records management program.
- Implement corrective actions to address identified issues.
- Continuously improve the records management program through monitoring, measurement, and review.

Given next are three examples of how this standard can apply to the activities and compliance requirements of research libraries:

- *Appraisal and selection of records*: Research libraries need to regularly evaluate the value of the records that they acquire and must ensure that these records are relevant to their policy and purpose. For example, when deciding whether to acquire a collection of personal papers or digital materials, the library must consider the value of the records for research purposes, their physical condition, and any legal or ethical issues associated with their acquisition.

- *Access and security*: Research libraries must ensure that the records that they hold in their collection remain secure and accessible only to authorized users. To accomplish this goal, they must implement and maintain appropriate security measures, such as access controls, monitoring, and audit trails, and must also provide access to the records solely in accordance with their stated policies and their legal or contractual requirements.

- *Preservation and retention*: Research libraries have an obligation, as set forth in retention policies that are based on applicable law, to preserve and retain records for as long as they are needed for research, cultural, or legal purposes. To accomplish this goal, they must implement a preservation strategy that includes identifying the records that need to be kept and the period for which those records must be kept (and, as required, destroyed, and must also ensure their physical and digital preservation and facilitate their long-term physical access by library users. This is in addition to the general duty to comply with legal or contractual requirements governing the retention and disposal of records.

Despite the centrality of this standard, as with other IG priorities such as training, policies, and procedures, just having standards is far from sufficient to realize the goals of IG. While standards help and guide the business processes and the work of records and archives management, to be effective, they must be well embedded into business, technical, and other broader information and records management policies. This requires knowledge workers such as librarians to coordinate across various divergent disciplines and domains, including IT, risk management, HR, legal, and information management.[10]

A closely related standard, ISO/TR 21965:2019, provides guidelines for the development and implementation of digital records policies. These guidelines cover all aspects of digital records management, including:

- *Record creation*: How to create digital records, including standards for metadata and file formats
- *Capture*: How to capture digital records, including best practices for scanning, digitizing, and born-digital records
- *Retention*: How organizations should retain digital records, including determining retention periods and ensuring secure storage
- *Disposal*: How organizations should dispose of records, including policies and procedures determining how they should delete, destroy, or transfer records
- *Access and use*: How entities should ensure access to digital records, including policies for searchability and retrieval and policies to ensure that access is granted based on regulatory requirements
- *Preservation*: How organizations should preserve digital records over time, including strategies for maintaining file integrity, migrating records to new formats, and ensuring long-term access to records

Another important standard is ISO 22428, which focuses on the management of digital records in digital format that are stored within cloud computing environments. ISO 22428 provides a set of guidelines to allow organizations to effectively manage their digital records throughout their life cycle, ensuring their authenticity, integrity, and accessibility, and addresses various aspects of cloud-based digital records management, including the creation, capture, classification, storage, retrieval, and preservation of records.

---

[10] Microsoft Word – DLM Forum 2005_paper_Hofman.doc (interpares.org).

In addition to ISO 15489, the related standards include ISO 16175, which focuses on the principles and functional requirements for records in electronic office environments; ISO 23081, which addresses various principles and practices of managing records in an information system environment; ISO 14721 (OAIS), which outlines the reference model for an Open Archival Information System (OAIS) for the long-term preservation and access to digital information; and ISO 16363, which addresses matters such as the assessment and certification of trustworthy digital repositories.

In the context of libraries managing and protecting their archives and user data in a cloud environment, ISO 22428 offers libraries a framework to establish robust digital records management practices, so that they can more effectively promote their preservation of important archival materials and protect user data. Specifically, it helps libraries to implement systematic processes for organizing and categorizing records, which make it easier for users and staff to locate and retrieve specific documents when needed. It also provides guidelines to libraries seeking to promote the authenticity and integrity of their records, which is crucial for maintaining the trustworthiness and reliability of library archives, and helps libraries to implement appropriate cloud security measures such as encryption, access controls, and data backup.

From a risk management standpoint, following these guidelines can help libraries avoid certain common pitfalls associated with data loss risks. The standard does this by providing guidance, which can be implemented within library training materials, on implementing effective backup strategies and disaster recovery plans, minimizing the chances of data loss in an attack. The standard also promotes data privacy compliance by providing a set of recommendations that emphasize the importance of proper access controls and data encryption techniques, which, if followed, can reduce the likelihood of human error. Finally, the standard includes a robust framework for preservation planning, which can be critical for libraries seeking to ensure the integrity and accessibility of their archives over extended periods by implementing sustainable preservation strategies that mitigate the risk of format obsolescence or data decay.

ISO 16175-1:2020—Information and Documentation—Processes and Functional Requirements for Software for Managing Records— Part 1: Functional Requirements and Associated Guidance for Any Applications That Manage Digital Records[11]

ISO Standard 16175-1 establishes fundamental principles and functional requirements for software that is used create and manage digital information in office environments. Core elements of the standard include:

- Guiding principles, best practices, implementation guidelines and also provides an overview of risks and measures.
- The application provides improved support for auditing activities in the field of automated information capture.
- Supporting good governance (e.g., accountability, transparency, and better service) through good archive management.
- Maximizing consistency between different jurisdictions when formulating functional requirements for managing records.
- Principles and functional requirements for archives in electronic office environments.

From an IG standpoint, the standard helps organizations to:

- Review their information and records management functionality and to assess the compliance of existing systems.
- Identify information and records management functionalities that should be included in the design specification for building, upgrading, or selecting new systems.
- Isolate the principles and functional requirements that enable them to better manage their business information through:
  - Supporting business needs by enabling greater effectiveness and efficiency of processing.

---

[11] ISO 16175 Standard for digital archiving – May 2022 – (itpedia.nl)

o Promoting greater accountability, transparency, and improved service.

o Improving the general awareness of the automation capabilities for archives and records management,

o Creating a foundation for government agencies, national archives, and the wider information management profession to engage with existing and new software vendors.

It is important to note that the functional requirements set forth in the standard are based on what the formulators considered to be the minimum requirements for records functionality—and, as a result, the standard contains no specifications for the long-term storage of digital documents.

ISO 16175-1:2020 specifies the requirements for recordkeeping functionality, including the capture, maintenance, and disposition of digital records, and the metadata required to support these functions.

Some of the main clauses in the standard include the following.

Clause 5: General functional requirements: These requirements ensure that digital records are properly managed throughout their life cycle, from creation to disposal, in a secure and reliable manner. The clause provides guidance on how software applications should be designed to meet these functional requirements. Main themes of this clause include:

- *Records management policy and framework*: This clause emphasizes the importance of having a records management policy and framework in place to provide guidance and direction for records management activities.
- *Roles and responsibilities*: The standard requires organizations to define and assign roles and responsibilities for records management, including the appointment of a records manager or records management team.
- *Risk management*: This clause emphasizes the importance of assessing and managing risks related to records management, including risks related to the security, confidentiality, and integrity of records.

- *Performance measurement*: The standard requires organizations to establish metrics and measures to evaluate the effectiveness of their records management program and to use these metrics to drive continuous improvement.
- *Business requirements*: This clause emphasizes the importance of understanding and aligning records management activities with business requirements, including the organization's mission, vision, and goals.
- *Legal and regulatory requirements*: This clause requires organizations to comply with legal and regulatory requirements related to records management, including requirements related to data privacy, retention, and disposal.
- *Organizational culture*: The standard emphasizes the importance of organizational culture in supporting effective records management, including the need for a culture of accountability, transparency, and information sharing.
- *Stakeholder needs*: This clause requires organizations to consider the needs and expectations of stakeholders in the development and implementation of their records management program.
- *Continuous improvement*: The standard requires organizations to establish processes for continuous improvement of their records management program, including regular monitoring and review of records management processes.
- *Integration with other management systems*: This clause emphasizes the importance of integrating records management with other management systems, including quality management, information security management, and environmental management.
- *Monitoring and review of records management processes*: The standard requires organizations to establish processes for monitoring and reviewing their records management program, including regular audits and evaluations.
- *Access to records*: This clause requires organizations to establish policies and procedures for providing access to records, while

ensuring the confidentiality, privacy, and security of sensitive information.

- *Security of records*: This clause emphasizes the importance of ensuring the security of records throughout their life cycle, including during storage, retrieval, and disposal.
- *Preservation of records*: The standard requires organizations to establish policies and procedures for the preservation of records, including the use of appropriate storage and handling practices.
- *Record retention schedules*: This clause requires organizations to establish record retention schedules that specify the length of time that records should be kept, based on legal, regulatory, and business requirements.
- *Records disposition and disposal*: The standard requires organizations to establish policies and procedures for the disposition and disposal of records, including the secure destruction of sensitive information.
- *Records management training and awareness*: This clause emphasizes the importance of providing training and awareness programs to employees to ensure that they understand the importance of records management and their role in the organization's records management program.

Clause 6: Records management functional requirements: This clause provides more detailed functional requirements for records. Specific elements of the clause include:

- *Identification*: This clause describes the process of identifying records and ensuring that they are properly managed throughout their life cycle. This includes identifying records that are created or received by the organization, as well as those that are obtained from external sources.
- *Capture*: This clause outlines the methods and processes for capturing records, including the use of digital technologies and the importance of maintaining the integrity and authenticity of records.

- *Classification*: This clause describes the process of classifying records, including the use of metadata schemas to describe the content and context of records. The standard emphasizes the importance of using standardized metadata schemas to ensure interoperability and long-term access to records.
- *Storage*: This clause outlines the requirements for storing records, including the need for secure and reliable storage systems and the importance of ensuring that records are properly indexed and searchable.
- *Access*: This clause describes the requirements for providing access to records, including the need for access controls to ensure the confidentiality, privacy, and security of sensitive information.
- *Disposition*: This clause outlines the requirements for the disposition of records, including the development of retention and disposition schedules that specify the length of time that records should be kept, based on legal, regulatory, and business requirements.
- *Metadata*: This clause emphasizes the importance of metadata in records management, including the need for standardized metadata schemas to ensure interoperability and long-term access to records. The standard provides guidance on the use of metadata for record identification, capture, classification, storage, access, and disposition.
- *Version control*: This clause describes the requirements for version control, including the need for clear and consistent version numbering and the maintenance of a record of changes.
- *Retention and disposition schedules*: This clause provides guidance on the development of retention and disposition schedules, including the need to consider legal, regulatory, and business requirements, as well as the potential long-term value of records.
- *Audit trails*: This clause describes the importance of maintaining audit trails to track the creation, use, and disposition of records, as well as the need for regular audits of records management processes to ensure compliance with legal, regulatory, and organizational requirements.

Clause 7: Design and implementation guidance: This clause offers guidance on designing and implementing software applications that meet the functional requirements outlined in Clauses 5 and 6. This includes guidance on system architecture, database design, user interfaces, and system testing and evaluation.

Clause 8: Appraisal and selection of software applications: This clause provides guidance on how organizations can evaluate and select software applications that meet their specific records management needs. This includes guidance on assessing vendor capabilities, conducting product evaluations, and performing system testing and validation.

Clause 9: Implementation and operation: This clause provides guidance on implementing and operating software applications for managing digital records. This includes guidance on system configuration, user training, and ongoing system monitoring and maintenance.

Clause 10: Integration with other systems: This clause provides guidance on integrating records management software with other systems and applications, including guidance on interoperability, data exchange formats, and integration testing.

Clause 11: Legal and regulatory requirements: This clause outlines the legal and regulatory requirements that must be considered when implementing software applications for managing digital records. This includes requirements related to data privacy, security, and retention, in addition to requirements related to data protection and access rights, intellectual property laws, and sector-specific requirements.

Clause 12: Records management policies and procedures: This clause provides guidance on developing and implementing records management policies and procedures that support the use of software applications for managing digital records. This includes guidance on developing policies for record creation, retention and disposition, access controls, and audit trails.

Examples of how the aforementioned clauses could apply to libraries might include:

A research library that is implementing a new system for managing digital archives could use the functional requirements outlined in Clauses 5 and 6 to ensure that the system meets its specific needs for metadata management, record classification, retention and disposition, and security and access controls.

A library uses this standard to ensure that digital records created as part of digitization projects are managed in compliance with the requirements for digital recordkeeping. This can include capturing and maintaining metadata associated with the digitized materials, ensuring that digital records are disposed of in accordance with retention schedules and maintaining the authenticity and integrity of the digital records.

Libraries use the standard to ensure that digital records created or acquired for preservation purposes are managed in compliance with the requirements for digital recordkeeping. This can include ensuring that digital records are preserved in formats that are sustainable over time, that metadata required for long-term preservation is captured and maintained, and that appropriate disposition and disposal strategies are in place for digital records that are no longer required.

A library using the standard ensures that electronic records created or received in the course of their business operations are managed in compliance with the requirements for digital recordkeeping. This can include capturing and maintaining metadata associated with electronic records, ensuring that electronic records are disposed of in accordance with retention schedules, and maintaining the authenticity and integrity of the electronic records.

ISO/TS 16175-2:2020—Information and Documentation—Processes and Functional Requirements for Software for Managing Records— Part 2: Guidance for Selecting, Designing, Implementing and Maintaining Software for Managing Records

ISO/TS 16175-2:2020 provides guidance on implementing software for managing records, with the following main elements:

- *Assessing the context of the organization*: This involves understanding the internal and external factors that affect the organization's records management, such as legal and regulatory requirements, organizational culture, and technology infrastructure.

- *Scoping the project*: This involves defining the scope of the software implementation project, including the records to be managed, the stakeholders involved, and the technical requirements of the software.
- *Identifying requirements for software functionality*: This involves identifying the specific requirements for the software functionality, such as conversion and migration requirements, security and access controls, and metadata management.
- *Communication, training, and change management*: This involves developing a communication plan to keep stakeholders informed throughout the implementation process, providing training to users on the new software, and managing the changes to processes and workflows resulting from the implementation.
- *Postimplementation review*: This involves reviewing the implementation process to assess its effectiveness, identifying areas for improvement, and making recommendations for future projects.

When defining the scope of a project, an organization should conduct an initial assessment of resources and capacity that are likely to impact the project. And, in particular, for example, when a library system is evaluating various software solutions for managing records, these criteria may include:

- *Business context*: For example, academic libraries that are part of a state university system can be required to follow jurisdictionwide rules. These strategic directions may impact options available for implementation. For example, a jurisdiction may require use of open source software or the use of a private government cloud, or a management direction may already have established a "cloud-first" policy, or that existing platform software will be used, or a specific software may be dictated by other organizational purchases. These management decisions frame what technology

directions the organization can take and in turn, may define
the parameters in which implementation of software for
managing records can take place.

- *IT infrastructure and networks*: Software for managing records,
  especially those that incorporate digitized images, can be
  very resource-intensive. Libraries need to consider their IT
  infrastructure and network capabilities in terms of network
  speed, bandwidth, storage capacity, and resolution available
  on user screens, to ensure that they can handle the additional
  volume and size of information.

- *Software scalability*: The extent to which software for
  managing records may need to "scale up" to larger or
  organizationwide deployment needs to be considered and
  planned for at an early stage in the implementation of
  software, to meet the library's business needs. Libraries should
  ensure that the software can accommodate growth and
  changes in business needs and records requirements.

- Software performance: Software for managing records, like
  all technology systems, need to define appropriate software
  performance parameters. Establishing appropriate software
  system performance criteria will define the necessary
  technology resources for performance-critical business
  processes to run smoothly. Performance criteria should be
  developed by taking into account the functional requirements
  and metadata requirements of records processes and records
  controls to meet organizational records requirements.

- *Budget*: All costs associated with implementing the
  software should be identified, including costs for selection,
  configuration, change management, and training associated
  with initial implementation. Ongoing costs should also be
  identified and assigned beyond a specific project budget
  allocation, such as ongoing training and support.

Given next are several use cases that illustrate good versus bad
practices related to this standard.

Use Case 1 (Good Practice)

A library is implementing software for managing records and takes into account the strategic directions established by governing bodies and funding agencies. They carefully consider the library's IT infrastructure and network capabilities, ensuring that they can handle the additional volume and size of information. They plan for the software's scalability, considering the library's potential for growth and changes in business needs and records requirements. They establish appropriate software system performance criteria based on the functional requirements and metadata requirements of records processes and records controls to meet organizational records requirements. Finally, they identify all costs associated with implementing the software, including ongoing costs for training and support.

Use Case 2 (Bad Practice)

A library implements software for managing records without considering the strategic directions established by governing bodies and funding agencies. They do not assess their IT infrastructure and network capabilities, leading to system failures and crashes. They do not plan for the software's scalability, resulting in a system that cannot accommodate growth and changes in business needs and records requirements. They do not establish appropriate software system performance criteria, leading to unpredictable software behavior. Finally, they do not identify all costs associated with implementing the software, leading to unexpected expenses and inadequate training and support.

CHAPTER 33

Information Governance by Design

Information governance by design is a proactive approach that integrates information governance principles into the design, development, and implementation of information systems and processes. This concept emphasizes the importance of considering information governance requirements from the early stages of system design, ensuring that data privacy, security, compliance, and records management considerations are embedded into the design and functionality of information systems. The ultimate goal is to help organizations, like libraries, to establish a solid foundation for effective information management, enabling them to meet legal, regulatory, and operational requirements while minimizing risks associated with poor information governance.

This concept is closely related to the approach of Privacy by Design, formulated by Dr. Ann Cavoukian, the former Information and Privacy Commissioner of Ontario, Canada, in the 1990s. The Privacy by Design formulation was borne out of a response to growing concerns about privacy in an interconnected world and encourages organizations to embed privacy-conscious practices into the design and operation of their systems and user interfaces, with the goal of considering privacy throughout the entire information life cycle.

The following figure explains some of the critical concepts of information governance by design.

ISO/TR 26122:2008, in particular, contains a series of useful, but nonbinding guidelines to promote the integration of recordkeeping requirements into an organization's business processes, emphasizing that recordkeeping considerations should be taken into account right from the early stages of process design and development. The purpose of this integration is to ensure that recordkeeping elements, such as metadata

Information Governance by Design

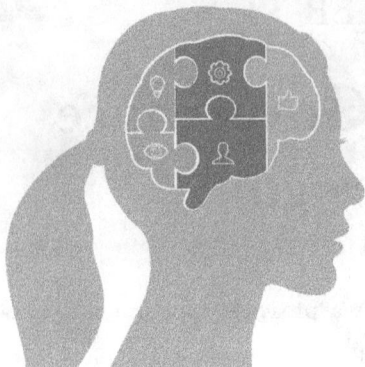

Information Governance by Design
means implementing G practices at the earliest stages into your organizational processes, instead of attempting to retrofit them later.

In other words, Preventative IG!

Planning
- Does your IG plan align with your broader business goals?
- Do you have enough corporate support? Project management?

Security and Privacy
- Do you have sufficient access controls?
- Do you have sufficient IT safeguards?

Data Architecture
Are your data systems scalable, flexible, and able to handle large amounts or data?

Compliance Culture
- Do you emphasize continual training?
- Policies and procedures adaptation, development and testing?

Policies and Procedures
Do your policies and procedures adequately define how you need to create, store, use, and dispose of information (and are they legally up-to-date)

(descriptive information about records), retention schedules (timeframes for retaining records), and other relevant requirements, are effectively incorporated into an organization's workflows and systems.

In the context of library management, this integration of recordkeeping requirements aligns with the broad concept of information governance by design. Information governance by design refers to the practice of proactively incorporating information governance principles, including recordkeeping, into the design and implementation of information systems and processes. By considering recordkeeping requirements early on, libraries can ensure that their management of information, including archival materials and user data, adheres to recognized standards and best practices.

For libraries, these factors include guidelines related to the creation and capture of records, the establishment of appropriate metadata standards for cataloging and organizing materials, and the implementation of retention and disposal schedules for effective life cycle management. By integrating recordkeeping requirements into the design and development of library processes, libraries can achieve greater consistency, accuracy, and transparency in their recordkeeping practices. This, in turn, enables libraries to increase the likelihood that their collections, archives, and user data are managed in a manner that aligns with industry standards, legal requirements, and best practices, while minimizing risks associated with inadequate recordkeeping.

Perhaps more importantly, the ISO 30300 series of standards supports the implementation of information governance by design by providing organizations with a framework and guidelines for establishing effective records management systems. The overarching goal of these standards is to help organizations instill information governance principles into their system design, thereby ensuring compliance, data protection, and efficient management of records and information assets.

ISO 30301:2011—Management Systems for Records—Requirements addresses important project planning elements including policy development, accountability, records classification and retention, access controls, and monitoring of the records management system's performance. The goal of this standard is to enable organizations to plan, develop, and establish a robust and compliant records management system based on information governance best practices.

In the project planning stage, this allows libraries, prior to implementing records management systems, to develop comprehensive information governance best-practice policies, assign clear project management roles and responsibilities, plan and institute effective records classification and retention practices, establish appropriate access controls, and monitor system performance to promote compliance, protect personally identifiable information, and maintain the integrity of records.

ISO 30302: Project Planning provides organizations such as libraries with a further series of useful guidelines to help them effectively and thoroughly address records management requirements, objectives, and resources before implementing a records management system.

This standard recommends:

- Developing a project plan that describes the proposed project scope, milestones, tasks, responsibilities, and timelines.
- Involving key stakeholders throughout the implementation process, which should include a steering committee composed of representatives from various departments or functional areas such as IT personnel, risk management, regulatory personnel, records management, finance, legal counsel, and general management (which can include HR). The purpose of

this group (and the reason why it must be broad based) is to allow the organization to gather valuable input, ensure buy-in, and align the records management system with organizational needs, goals, and specific pain points, in addition to allowing staff the critical chance to "be heard."

- Conducting a thorough risk assessment to identify potential risks and vulnerabilities related to records management systems such as risks related to data privacy, security, compliance, and litigation, and develop and document mitigation strategies to address these risks.

- Allocating sufficient resources, including high-level executive support, personnel, technology, and financial resources, to enable and support the successful implementation and ongoing management of the records management system. In particular, this process should be led by a project manager and supported by specifically designated staff who will be responsible for implementing records management processes into the system, providing training and support, and ensuring the availability of necessary hardware, software, and infrastructure.

- Providing comprehensive training to employees to generate awareness about the records management system, including how to use the system; the policies, procedures, and best practices for safely, compliantly, and efficiently managing records through the system; and their roles and responsibilities in the process.

- Continual improvement and audit including regularly monitoring and evaluating system performance from both an information governance perspective and a system performance perspective, conducting regular audits, and soliciting feedback from stakeholders.

The figure is a summary of what we see as some of the primary structural elements of information governance by design:

What Are the Elements of IG by Design?

Built-In Policies, Procedures, Collaboration, and Disaster Recovery		
Information security and records management	Legal and regulatory and life cycle procedures	Incident management, breach reporting, and escalation
Retention schedule and archiving	Data receipt, classification, and collaboration	Backup and disaster recovery
Data privacy and remote working	Information volume and ROT removal	Confidentiality management
Regular Continuity and Auditing, Measurement, and Review		
KPI establishment and goal planning	Training, continuity, and update of policies	
Role allocation and internal audit	Information governance review, monitoring of information access and use, regulatory compliance, effectiveness of information security policies, future support review, and budgeting	

In a library with good information governance by design:

- Data privacy and protection are prioritized through legally compliant consent mechanisms and the use of appropriate, best-practice IT security methods.
- Systems are planned with consistent metadata standards that facilitate the effective retention of records and data and that align their records management requirements with retention and disposal schedules, and systematic archiving.
- The library works with its legal counsel and IT team to stay proactively updated on legal and regulatory requirements and to ensure the compliance of staff, users, and systems, through policies and procedures.
- Useful staff training and awareness programs are conducted and updated regularly to align with best practices and current legal standards.
- Role allocation and audit is conducted on a regular and scheduled periodic basis, to ensure system continuity and compliance.

The figure shows what it looks like!

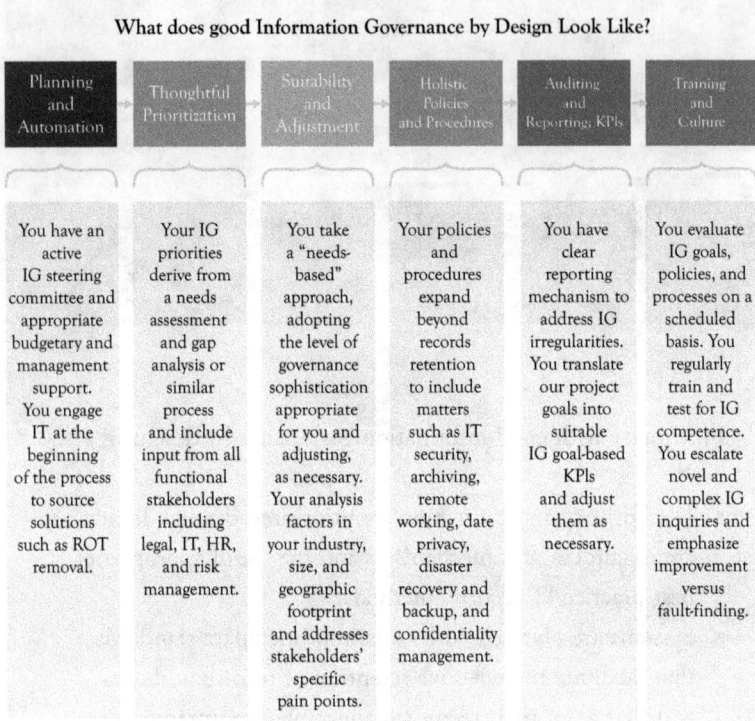

What does good Information Governance by Design Look Like?

Planning and Automation	Thoughtful Prioritization	Suitability and Adjustment	Holistic Policies and Procedures	Auditing and Reporting: KPIs	Training and Culture
You have an active IG steering committee and appropriate budgetary and management support. You engage IT at the beginning of the process to source solutions such as ROT removal.	Your IG priorities derive from a needs assessment and gap analysis or similar process and include input from all functional stakeholders including legal, IT, HR, and risk management.	You take a "needs-based" approach, adopting the level of governance sophistication appropriate for you and adjusting, as necessary. Your analysis factors in your industry, size, and geographic footprint and addresses stakeholders' specific pain points.	Your policies and procedures expand beyond records retention to include matters such as IT security, archiving, remote working, date privacy, disaster recovery and backup, and confidentiality management.	You have clear reporting mechanism to address IG irregularities. You translate our project goals into suitable IG goal-based KPIs and adjust them as necessary.	You evaluate IG goals, policies, and processes on a scheduled basis. You regularly train and test for IG competence. You escalate novel and complex IG inquiries and emphasize improvement versus fault-finding.

In summary, libraries that integrate information governance by design principles can promote a planned culture of information governance compliance and best standards, safeguard their valuable collections, better protect user privacy, and validate how their regulatory resources are spent.

CHAPTER 34

Privacy Considerations Impacting Libraries

Introduction

The primary goal of all libraries (including research libraries and corporate libraries) is to store and organize information so that users can access it. And to meet their primary mission, libraries must ensure that the atmosphere they provide does not discourage patrons from investigating any subject that they found of interest.[1]

As a result, and consistent with international standards, the American Library Association's (ALA) privacy policy document recognizes privacy as a fundamental right. The ALA sees library users' freedom to choose, access, and utilize library resources as being negatively affected by a lack of privacy and confidentiality and, conversely, it sees the zealous protection of user privacy rights as a cornerstone of the general fundamental right to free speech.[2]

According to the ALA policy, everyone, including children and youth, has a right to privacy in their lawful library use, and libraries should safeguard their personally identifiable information and library use data from any unauthorized access or surveillance. Moreover, according to the ALA, library policies or practices should never infringe on users' privacy rights, regardless of their personal attributes, unless

---

[1] Chapter 8, Engaging Privacy and Information Technology in a Digital Age (2007), James Waldo, Herbert S. Lin, and Lynette I. Millett, Editors; Committee on Privacy in the Information Age; Computer Science and Telecommunications Board; Division on Engineering and Physical Sciences; National Research Council.

[2] www.ala.org/advocacy/intfreedom/librarybill/interpretations/privacy.

required by law, and consultation with legal counsel should occur before any such action is taken.[3]

Libraries like other institutions, and particularly, institutions whose activities impact constitutional rights such as free speech, have a duty to inform users of policies and practices regarding the collection, security, and retention of personally identifiable information and library use data.

To satisfy current privacy standards, these rights should include an option by library users to opt in to nonessential data collection and to opt out at any time, with nonessential data collection turned off by default. Moreover, in order to comply with applicable privacy laws, best librarianship practices emphasize prioritizing user control over their privacy choices, including in the context of the selection, access, and use of information. Users should be informed of their options in a clear and accessible manner.

In terms of internal policies, librarians have a longstanding commitment to facilitating access to information, rather than monitoring it. In the modern privacy context, this commitment requires implementing best-practice library privacy policies that are up-to-date and consistent with applicable laws and regulations including federal, state, local, and international laws where applicable. Such policies must be publicly available and outline what data is being collected, with whom it is shared, and how long it is kept. Everyone involved in library governance, administration, or service, including volunteers, has a responsibility to respect and protect the privacy of all users.

With respect to personal data collection, the U.S. National Information Standards Organization (NISO) Consensus Principles on Users' Digital Privacy in Library, Publisher, and Software-Provider Systems recognizes the importance of users' privacy in library services. And, to this end, personal should only be collected with users' consent and for disclosed purposes.

Moreover, consistent with this standard, as a general rule, libraries should not monitor, track, or profile users beyond operational needs, and data collected for analytical purposes should be anonymous or aggregated. And the use of emerging biometric technologies, such as facial

---

[3] Id.

recognition, is considered by the ALA to be inconsistent with the goal of facilitating access to library resources free from intrusion or surveillance.

From a practical standpoint, adherence to proper privacy standards must also include the adoption of best-practices technological standards including encryption of personal data, prompt updates of systems and software, access control procedures for sensitive data, security training for those with data access, and documented procedures for breach reporting and incident response. Libraries must also adhere to the principles ensconced within comprehensive privacy laws including purpose limitation, storage limitation, and data minimization when collecting and retaining user data, and periodically review data collection policies to ensure they are still necessary.

Finally, and consistent with such laws, unless mandated by applicable law, libraries should never share users' personally identifiable information with third parties or vendors without explicit user consent or legal requirements. And libraries should negotiate agreements with vendors that retain library ownership of user data and allow independent auditing of vendor data policies. And law enforcement requests for library records should be handled through a proper procedure and court order.

This chapter addresses a number of the core principles and practices that are incumbent upon libraries that relate to privacy protection.

The Importance of Privacy Laws

Privacy laws are extremely important to libraries because they protect the privacy of library users and allow libraries to fulfill their mission of providing free access to information.

These laws protect the personal information of library users, such as their borrowing history and online activity, and ensure that this data is not disclosed without their consent or a court order. In addition, libraries collect and maintain sensitive information about their patrons, including their reading habits, research interests, and other personal details, some of which may be subject to additional legal protections such as protections based on the disclosure of health data, racial origin, or sexual orientation. By strictly adhering to privacy laws, libraries can help to ensure that this information remains confidential and is not subject to unauthorized access, use, or disclosure.

In contrast, a failure to adequately safeguard privacy can create a chilling effect on the ability of library users to access needed information. Libraries must ensure their users that their information will be kept private and secure to encourage them to use library services without fear of judgment or reprisal. And if library users believe that their personal information may be used or disclosed without their permission, they may be hesitant to use library services, which can have a negative impact on the library's ability to fulfill its mission and on users' ability to access needed information.

Finally, libraries face a significant challenge in safeguarding the anonymity and privacy of their patrons, particularly given the crucial role of libraries in serving the interests of students, educational institutions, and marginalized communities. And library literature reflects a strong concern for protecting patron privacy, including on social media platforms, against behavioral data surveillance, and from government institutions.[4]

Important U.S. laws that apply to libraries include the following:

The U.S. Privacy Act of 1974

The Privacy Act of 1974 regulates how government agencies, including libraries that receive federal funding, collect, use, and disclose personal information. The act impacts libraries that receive federal funding and includes many public libraries, academic libraries, public sector libraries, and research libraries.

Most importantly, the act provides specific limitations and instructions on how libraries can collect, use, and disclose personal information. Personal information is defined in the act as any information that identifies an individual, including their name, address, social security number, and other identifiable details.

Libraries covered by the act must:

- Inform individuals when their personal information is collected and how it will be used.
- Keep accurate records and adequately safeguard the personal information they collect.

---

[4] petsymposium.org/popets/2023/popets-2023-0064.pdf.

- Allow individuals to access and amend their personal information.
- Obtain individuals' consent before disclosing their personal information to third parties.
- Provide individuals with the ability to file a complaint if their privacy rights are violated.

The provisions of this act are generally consistent with the general principles of most comprehensive privacy laws. While these laws can differ in substance, the primary elements of these laws are as follows:

What Do Comprehensive Privacy Laws Look Like?

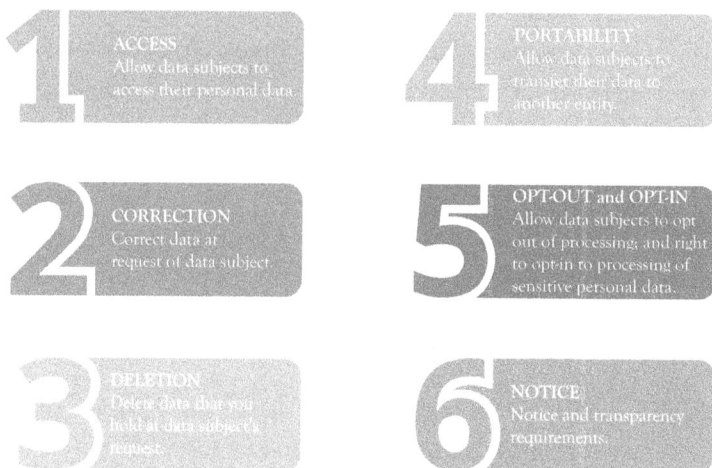

1. ACCESS Allow data subjects to access their personal data.

4. PORTABILITY Allow data subjects to transfer their data to another entity.

2. CORRECTION Correct data at request of data subject.

5. OPT-OUT and OPT-IN Allow data subjects to opt out of processing; and right to opt-in to processing of sensitive personal data.

3. DELETION Delete data that you hold at data subject's request.

6. NOTICE Notice and transparency requirements.

Source: Adapted from "2021 Proposed comprehensive US privacy legislation," IAPP.

Electronic Communications Privacy Act (ECPA)

Another important law is the Electronic Communications Privacy Act (ECPA), which protects the privacy of electronic communications, including e-mail and Internet usage. This act prohibits the interception, access, and disclosure of electronic communications without a warrant or the user's consent. In contrast to the Privacy Act of 1974, the ECPA applies to all types of libraries, including those that do not receive federal funding.

The ECPA prohibits libraries from intercepting, accessing, or disclosing electronic communications without obtaining the explicit consent of the user or as authorized by applicable law. The law also includes penalties to deter libraries from engaging in the unauthorized interception or disclosure of electronic communications, including fines and imprisonment.

Importantly, before disclosing the contents of electronic communications, the ECPA requires libraries to obtain a court order, except in limited circumstances, such as if the user has given explicit consent.

Children's Online Privacy Protection Act (COPPA)

The Children's Online Privacy Protection Act (COPPA) regulates how websites and online services collect, use, and disclose personal information from children under the age of 13. Although the law does not specifically target libraries, it is likely to impact many libraries, particularly those that collect personal information of children such as names, addresses, and e-mails to register them for activities or online educational resources. Libraries subject to COPPA are likely to need to obtain verifiable parental consent before collecting personal information from children under 13 and must also provide parents with the ability to review and delete their child's personal information.

Family Educational Rights and Privacy Act (FERPA)

Another federal law that is likely to impact certain libraries, particularly those that are affiliated with educational institutions, is Family Educational Rights and Privacy Act (FERPA). This law mandates that educational institutions must protect the privacy of student education records, and includes records that are kept by libraries at such institutions.

U.S. State Laws

Confidentiality of library records is protected by laws in 48 states and the District of Columbia, with Kentucky and Hawaii having attorney generals' opinions to safeguard library users' privacy. While the precise language of these laws varies from state to state, most of these laws stipulate that library users' information and records are confidential and cannot be disclosed unless certain conditions are met.

To adhere to best practices, however, the ALA advises libraries to create a policy that recognizes the confidentiality of information obtained from users, including personally identifiable information, and acknowledges the state confidentiality provisions.

This policy should also acknowledge the confidentiality of any records or electronic data that reveals the materials consulted, borrowed, or acquired by a user, which may include online search histories, circulation records, and interlibrary loan records. Libraries should also have procedures in place for handling law enforcement requests for records and should disclose such records only in accordance with library policy and the law.[5]

Legal Challenges Facing U.S. Librarians—USA Patriot Act and DMCA

The USA Patriot Act poses a number of challenges to librarians related to privacy and surveillance. This act grants the federal government broad powers to access library records and monitor the activities of library users in the name of national security. One of the major challenges that librarians face is how to balance a free access to information with their legal requirement to provide patron information and records to authorities without a patron's knowledge or consent, which undermines the principles of intellectual freedom and privacy that libraries strive to uphold.

Librarians face further challenges under the Digital Millennium Copyright Act (DMCA), related to copyright infringement and digital content. The DMCA prohibits persons from circumventing technological protection measures used by content creators to safeguard copyrighted materials. This results in librarians being required to navigate the complex landscape of digital rights management and fair use to ensure compliance with copyright law while, at the same time, providing access to information and preserving the rights of library users.

From a compliance perspective, it has become increasingly important for libraries to provide their staff with robust training about the requirements of these laws and of any legal rights that they may have. Libraries

---

[5] www.ala.org/advocacy/privacy/statelaws.

should also draft and institute clear policies and procedures related to these laws and, specifically, outlining how they handle patrons' information. Another important protection is to institute technical measures to protect against digital rights infringement, reflecting their commitment to both information governance and Privacy by Design.

International Standards

One important international standard is the IFLA Statement on Privacy in the Library Environment.[6] The statement is based on the general concept that the freedom of access to information and freedom of expression, as expressed in Article 19 of the Universal Declaration of Human Rights, are essential concepts for the library and information profession. Privacy is integral to ensuring these rights.

Libraries have a particular duty to protect users' personal data. This is because excessive data collection and use threatens individual users' privacy and has other social and legal consequences. When Internet users are aware of large-scale data collection and surveillance, they may self-censor their behavior due to the fear of unexpected consequences. Excessive data collection can then have a chilling effect on society, narrowing an individual's right to freedom of speech and freedom of expression as a result of this perceived threat. Limiting freedom of speech and expression has the potential to compromise democracy and civil engagement.

In addition, the statement notes that from a data collection perspective, users´ privacy in libraries has become widely challenged. Commercial content and service providers used by library and information services may collect data on users' activities, communications, and transactions or require that libraries collect data as a condition of providing their content or services. Cloud-based library systems may transfer and store users' data outside of the library or information service. When library and information services offer services on mobile devices, these services may collect identity and location data, track the use of the library or information service, and share the data with third parties.

---

[6] www.ifla.org/publications/ifla-statement-on-privacy-in-the-library-environment/.

Library and information services also often act as data controllers that make independent decisions about local system and data management. For example, library and information services can decide what kind of personal data they will collect on users and consider principles of data security, management, storage, sharing, and retention. They can also negotiate with commercial service providers to ensure the protection of users' privacy, refuse to acquire services that collect excessive data, or limit the use of technologies that could compromise users' privacy.

The statement offers specific privacy-oriented guidelines for libraries, which include the duties to:

- Respect and advance privacy both at the level of practices and as a principle.
- Support national-, regional-, and international-level advocacy efforts (e.g., by human rights and digital rights organizations) to protect individuals' privacy and their digital rights and encourage library professionals to reflect on these issues.
- Reject electronic surveillance and any type of illegitimate monitoring or collection of users' personal data or information behavior that would compromise their privacy and affect their rights to seek, receive, and impart information. Libraries should also take measures to limit collection of personal information about their users and the services that they use.
- Ensure that government intrusion in users' information or communications by the government is based on legitimate principles for such practices and necessary and proportionate to legitimate aims (e.g., described in "International Principles on the Application of Human Rights to Communications Surveillance").
- Encourage users to be aware of the implications and provide guidance in data protection and privacy protection.
- Support their users' ability to make informed choices, take legitimate actions, and weigh risks and benefits in their communications and use of services on the Internet.

- Include data protection instruction as a part of the media and information literacy training for library and information service users and include training on tools to use to protect their privacy.
- Educate library and information professionals on data and privacy protection principles and practices in a networked environment.

Privacy by Design and Privacy by Default

Privacy by Design and Privacy by Default are two important concepts in the field of data protection.

Generally, Privacy by Design means that organizations should consider privacy and data protection issues throughout the entire life cycle of a project, from its inception to its disposal. Entities implementing Privacy by Design must embed privacy principles, best practices, and safeguards into the design and architecture of information systems, rather than adding them as an afterthought.

Privacy by Default means that organizations should endeavor to implement the highest level of privacy settings into their default settings. Practically, this means that personal data should not be processed unless it is necessary for the specific purpose for which it is processed and that the entity's default settings are set to the most private options available. For example, a library website should set users' profiles to private by default, rather than public.

ISO 27701 emphasizes the importance of considering data protection regulations when developing and maintaining information security policies. This includes implementing systems and components in line with the principles of Privacy by Design and Privacy by Default. The standard also requires organizations to formulate a policy to contribute to Privacy by Design and Privacy by Default, as set forth in Clause 6.11.2.1.

ISO 27701's Controls A.7.4 and B.8.4, along with Clauses 7.4 and 8.4, emphasize that organizations must follow Privacy by Design and Privacy by Default principles when collecting and processing personal data. These principles include limiting collection, ensuring accuracy, minimizing data, and preventing reidentification of deleted personal data. Personally identifiable information processors should also ensure the secure disposal of personal data, periodically delete unused temporary files, and comply with customer contract requirements for data transfers.

In the context of research libraries, adhering to the principles of Privacy by Design and Privacy by Default means that when designing and implementing systems for handling personal data, such as user registration and authentication systems, libraries should take into account and apply the principles of Privacy by Design and Privacy by Default. For example, a library creating a system for tracking and managing borrowing histories should evaluate how it should minimize the collection and storage of unnecessary personal data. Library management should also ensure that privacy settings are set to the most protective defaults and that users of the system are provided with clear and concise information and instructions about how their personal data will be used and processed. Similarly, when implementing new technologies or services that involve the processing of personal data, libraries should prioritize privacy considerations from the outset, rather than trying to retrofit privacy measures at a later stage.

Data Subject Rights

Clause 7.3 and Control A.7.3 of ISO 27701 provide guidance for organizations including libraries on how they should respect the rights of data subjects. For example, libraries should identify, document, and provide information regarding their personal data processing activities. They should also verify that they can comply with statutory data subject rights and should provide a contact point that data subjects can use, which should be similar to the form used to collect personal data and consent (Clause 7.3.1 and Control A.7.3.1 of ISO 27701).

In addition to these measures, libraries and other organizations must identify, record, and update the timeframe and nature of information to be provided to data subjects. Also, any notices to data subjects must be clear, easily accessible, timely, concise, complete, transparent, intelligible, and in clear and plain language, taking the nature of the reader into account (Clause 7.3 and Control A.7.3 of ISO 27701).

An example of a notice that could meet this standard[7] is:

Dear Library User,

We value your privacy and are committed to protecting your personal data. This notice is to inform you about how we collect, use, and protect your personal data.

What personal data do we collect?

- Your name and contact information, such as your e-mail address and phone number
- Your borrowing history and preferences
- Your search history and use of library services

How do we use your personal data?

We may use your personal data to:

- Manage your library account and provide services to you.
- Improve our library services and resources.
- Communicate with you about library events, resources, and services.
- How do we protect your personal data?
- We take appropriate technical and organizational measures to protect your personal data from unauthorized access, disclosure, or misuse.

What rights do you have?

- You have the right to access, correct, and delete your personal data.
- You can also object to or restrict the processing of your personal data.

To exercise these rights or if you have any questions or concerns about how we process your personal data, please contact us at privacy@library.org.

---

[7] Various laws may require a more robust description of certain elements, and rights, for example, rights under the GDPR or CCPA, and the specific language should, ideally, be reviewed by a privacy lawyer.

Thank you for trusting us with your personal data.

Sincerely,
The Library Team

A use case for this principle, in the context of library management, could be when a library processes personal data of its patrons, such as their names and contact information for the purpose of library membership or checking out materials. The library in question must inform its patrons of their data processing rights, including their right to access, correct, and delete their personal data. The library must also regularly update its personal data processing activity records and verify that they are accurate and up-to-date.

Other important principles include:[8]

- The obligation to offer data subjects (such as library users) the option to object to processing, access, correct, or erase their personal data; withdraw or restrict consent; and be informed of their rights to do so at any time
- The duty to fulfill requests made by data subjects within a set period, as specified in the privacy policy
- The requirement to communicate changes to personal data to third parties
- The obligation to provide a copy of the personal data belonging to the data subject in a structured, commonly used format that allows the portability of the data to relevant parties
- The ability to charge reasonable fees for access requests under certain circumstances
- The obligation to follow jurisdiction-specific requirements for the automated processing of personal data, when applicable

---

[8] Clauses 6.7.1.1, 7.2.3, 7.3, and Controls A.7.2.3, A.7.3, 8.2.3 and Control B.8.2.3of ISO 27701.

- The requirement to provide information to the customer on the use of cryptography for data protection and the requirement to establish a clear procedure for obtaining consent from data subjects
- The obligation to obtain prior consent from data subjects for the processing of personal data under a contract for marketing purposes and to refrain from making the provision of services reliant on providing consent.

Given next are several use cases illustrating the aforementioned principles:

A library patron requests access to their borrowing history, which contains personal data such as their name and contact information. The library must provide this information in a structured format that is easily accessible to the patron and can be ported to other relevant parties if needed.

A library system automatically collects data on patron behavior, such as items borrowed and returned, and uses this information to personalize recommendations for future reading. Depending on the jurisdiction, the library may be required to notify patrons of this automated processing and obtain their consent. The library must verify any specific requirements regarding the automated processing of personal data and ensure that the notification and consent procedures are clearly defined and documented.

A library receives a subject access request from a patron who wants to know what personal data is being processed about them. The library must provide this information in a structured, commonly used format that is easily accessible to the patron and allows them to transfer it to relevant parties. The library may charge a fee for providing this information, depending on the jurisdiction.

A library wants to use a third-party marketing service to promote its services. Before doing so, the library must obtain the prior consent of patrons whose personal data will be used for this purpose. The library cannot make service provision dependent on providing consent. The library establishes a procedure for obtaining consent from patrons, determining when and how it will be obtained, and keeping a record of the consent received.

The Impact of Extraterritorial Privacy Laws

The European Union General Data Protection Regulation (GDPR) and European Union Law

According to analysis by the IFLA, the GDPR presents a number of unique challenges for libraries.[9]

These include:

- *Significant penalties.* Higher penalties of up to €20 million or 4 percent of global turnover can be levied for more serious infringements of core principles of the GDPR. For example, when a library relies on consent from an individual to use their personal information when registering at the library, the terms and conditions must clearly and in plain language explain how their information is being used.
- *Privacy by Design.* On a practical level, this means that libraries subject to the GDPR must proactively "design in" technical and organizational processes that comply with data protection law. For example, a library subject to the GDPR should not hold more personal information than is actually required or keep personal data for longer than is needed. It must ensure that its IT systems are safe also, and encryption or pseudonymization is strongly encouraged. Additionally, when a library plans new processes or IT systems, it should conduct an assessment measuring how the personal information being held by the library will be impacted.
- *Data breach.* If personal data has been lost, accessed unlawfully, or subject to a similar adverse event, libraries subject to the GDPR must inform authorities of the breach within 72 hours. People affected must also be told as soon as is practicable after the event took place unless the personal data has been encrypted.

---

[9] www.ifla.org/wp-content/uploads/2019/05/assets/clm/publications/briefing_general_data_protection_regulation_2018.pdf.

- *Rights of library patrons.* When a library is subject to the GDPR, persons using its systems have the right to be informed free of charge as to what information the library holds on them and for what purpose it is being used. They also (alongside a number of differing rights) have the right to be supplied a copy in electronic form of the data that the library holds on them and to require in many cases that data it holds on them is rectified, removed, or deleted from its systems.
- *Data protection officer.* All public authorities, which in many if not all European Union member states will include public, national, and university libraries, must appoint a data protection officer. A data protection officer can be shared with other organizations (e.g., with local government), but must be registered with the national data protection authority. Legally this person must not report to senior management and must have no conflict of interest in performing this role. For example, they should not be part of an IT department or report to a chief technology officer.

An additional issue impacting libraries subject to the GDPR is data transfer. Under the GDPR, the transfer of personal data outside the European Economic Area (EEA) is subject to strict rules to ensure the protection of individuals' personal data. These rules are applicable to all entities, including libraries, that process personal data within the EU and transfer it outside the EEA.

If a European Union library subject to the GDPR transfers personal data outside the EEA, it must ensure that the transfer complies with the GDPR data transfer rules. These rules require the library to provide appropriate safeguards to protect personal data transferred outside the EEA, such as standard contractual clauses (SCCs), binding corporate rules (BCRs), or obtaining explicit consent from the data subjects.

The GDPR also allows for the transfer of personal data outside the EEA without the need for additional safeguards if the European

Commission has deemed the destination country or organization to have an adequate level of data protection.

Therefore, EU libraries subject to the GDPR must carefully assess the legal basis for transferring personal data outside the EEA and ensure that they provide appropriate safeguards when necessary. And a failure to comply with these rules could result in significant fines and reputational damage.

The IFLA guideline offers a number of concrete compliance steps for libraries subject to the GDPR:

- The library should establish its legal basis for processing personal data and substantiate this basis. For example, a library that relies on consent to process personal data should document where it processes data based on a legal requirement, or as part of its public task as a public body. It should also establish whether it is processing personal data pursuant to a legal mandate or based on consent.
- When a library relies on consent for using personal information, it should first ensure that the terms and conditions that relate to using patrons' personal data are easily accessible (e.g., short and no legalese if possible) and understandable to an average person. The library should also ensure that they clearly explain exactly what it is using a patron's personal data for in plain language. And, finally, the library should make sure that the consent is a positive action—using pre-filled check boxes for example are not valid.
- Libraries subject to the GDPR must enact updated written records outlining the purpose for using personal data, the categories of personal data stored, time limits for deleting personal data, technical and organizational measures to protect personal data, and similar information. This information should be provided, on request, to library patrons, as well as to appropriate data protection authorities, on request.

If a library believes that its processing of personal data is subject to a GDPR exemption, it should consult with either its internal or external counsel or that of its parent institution. Possible exemptions include:

Freedom of expression and information exemptions. The GDPR allows European Union member states to introduce a wide variety of exemptions for freedom of expression and information purposes that may reduce many of the burdens the act imposes on libraries. In the section, in the regulation referring to freedom of expression and information, it specifically mentions news, broadcast, and press libraries. Because many libraries maintain archives of news and broadcast content and archives of a political nature, which are important for freedom of expression, the GDPR provides explicit grounds for exempting these libraries and archives from certain GDPR obligations on the basis that they play an important role in guaranteeing freedom of expression.

There may also be limited exemptions for organizations "archiving in the public interest," though some of these are not mandatory, so the member state can choose whether to pass them into law or not. Also, relying on this exemption may be more complicated as it requires that the library must also have a legal obligation "to acquire, preserve, appraise, arrange, describe, communicate, promote, disseminate and provide access to records of enduring value for general public interest."

Other potential nonmandatory exemptions include processing scientific or historical research purposes, as well as using personal data for statistical purposes. In any event, it is critical for libraries subject to the GDPR to verify with qualified counsel whether a particular exemption applies and whether its conduct is subject to an exemption.

The earlier analysis is relevant for libraries subject to the GDPR. Generally, the GDPR will apply to all libraries that process the personal data of European Union residents. This will include all libraries that are located within the EEA as well as certain libraries that process European Union personal data extraterritorially (e.g., through online systems that can be accessed from the European Union).[10]

---

[10] The GDPR defines personal data as any information that relates to an identified or identifiable natural person. This can include a person's name, identification number, location data, online identifier, or any other factors specific to the

To determine if a U.S. library is subject to the GDPR, three questions should be answered:

1. Does the library collect personal data?
2. Does it collect personal data relating to EU residents?
3. Does it use personal data of EU residents to offer goods or services or monitor their behavior in the EU?

On a basic level, therefore, if a library regularly offers goods or services that would be delivered in the EU, it must comply with the GDPR. Certain libraries are, therefore, more likely to be subject to the GDPR than others. For example, a large university research library is probably subject to the GDPR, if it processes the personal data of persons located within the European Union to provide them with research services. In contrast, a local public library may not.

Because of the complexity of these "basic" questions, however, if a library located outside of the European Union believes that it may be subject to the GDPR, it should obtain advice from qualified privacy counsel.

Other Extraterritorial Privacy Laws

A similar analysis would apply to the U.S. libraries assessing whether they are subject to other extraterritorial privacy laws such as the ones given in the following figure.

---

physical, physiological, genetic, mental, economic, cultural, or social identity of that person. Processing, according to the GDPR, means any operation or set of operations that is performed on personal data, whether or not by automated means, such as collection, recording, organization, structuring, storage, adaptation or alteration, retrieval, consultation, use, disclosure by transmission, dissemination or otherwise making available, alignment or combination, restriction, erasure, or destruction of personal data. Also, the GDPR applies to the processing of personal data of EU residents by controllers or processors not established in the EU, when the processing activities are related to offering goods or services to EU residents or monitoring their behavior within the EU. For instance, a U.S. company must comply with GDPR when processing personal data of EU residents accessed for the purpose of offering goods or services or monitoring their behavior in the EU.

Comprehensive Privacy Laws Are Worldwide

NORTH AMERICA

Laws include US: Numerous State comprehensive privacy laws such as the CCPA, the VCDPA, and the Colorado Data Privacy Act; NY's Shield Act; **Canada:** PIPEDA (Comprehensive—extraterritorial based on judicial interpretation); **Mexico:** Federal Law on the Protection of Personal Data held by Private Properties2010

SOUTH AMERICA

Laws include Argentina's Personal Data Protection Act 2000; **Brazilian** General Data Protection Law; Law 1581/12, Decree1377/13, Data Protection Act (**Uruguay**)

EUROPE

Laws include the GDPR, various member state regulations and interpretations; **Danish** Act on Data Protection 2018 Act (Law No.502 of May 23, 2018; Data Protection Act 2018 (HE 9/2018VP) (**Finland**); Processing of Personal Data (Act No. 90/2018) (**Iceland**); various sectoral laws and regulations

AFRICA

Protection of Personal Information (PoPI) Act 2013 (**South Africa**)

ASIA

Laws include Personal Data Protection Act (PDPA) (**Taiwan**); Personal Data Protection Act (2019) (PDPA) (**Thailand**); Act on the Protection of Personal Information (2003) (**Japan**); Personal Data Protection Act (2012) (**Singapore**); Proposed **Chinese** Personal Information Protection Law

AUSTRALIA

Privacy Act 1988 (**Australia**); Privacy Act 1993 (**New Zealand**)

CHAPTER 35

The Importance of Technical Security Measures

Historically, libraries have been one of the earliest adopters of technology. From the outset, libraries have used computer systems to increase the selection of resources that they can provide to users and to keep track of which consumers have checked out which products. And, given their core mission, the protection of users' privacy has been a consistent, top priority for libraries, which have, as a community, adopted a proactive stance in assessing the potential and privacy implications of new technologies, realizing that it is far more challenging to raise privacy concerns after a technology has been adopted.[1] The following subsections address several of the core technology privacy standards applicable to libraries.

ISO/IEC 27701—Security Techniques—Extension to ISO/IEC 27001 and ISO/IEC 27002 for Privacy Information Management—Requirements and Guidelines[2]

Introduction

ISO/IEC 27701 sets out the prerequisites and offers advice for creating, preserving, and continuously improving a privacy information

---

[1] Chapter 8, Engaging Privacy and Information Technology in a Digital Age (2007), James Waldo, Herbert S. Lin, and Lynette I. Millett, Editors; Committee on Privacy in the Information Age; Computer Science and Telecommunications Board; Division on Engineering and Physical Sciences; National Research Council.

[2] www.dataguidance.com/opinion/international-iso-27701. Most of the information on ISO 27701 is taken from this source.

management system (PIMS) that extends the PIMS implementation based on the criteria of ISO/IEC 27001 and the guidance of ISO/IEC 27002.

This standard is relevant to both personally identifiable information controllers and personally identifiable information processors. The additional guidelines and requirements for protecting personally identifiable information can be implemented by any organization, regardless of its size or cultural context.

ISO/IEC 27701 provides information on how to align this standard with the privacy framework and principles specified in ISO/IEC 29100. Additionally, it includes mapping to ISO/IEC 27018, ISO/IEC 29151, and GDPR. The first version of ISO 27701 was published on August 5, 2019.

Purpose of ISO 27701

ISO 27701 is an extension of ISO 27001 and ISO 27002 that establishes additional requirements and provides guidance for the safeguarding of privacy as potentially affected by personal data processing. These requirements and recommendations help entities to incorporate requirements regarding information security and protection of personal data into their general information security management systems.

Specifically, ISO 27701 details what is necessary for establishing, implementing, maintaining, and continually improving a personal information management system and offers guidance to organizations to enable the establishment, implementation, maintenance, and continual improvement of a personal information management systems and maintain the confidentiality, integrity, and availability ("CIA") of the personal data within those systems. ISO 27701 also references the privacy framework of ISO 29100.

The goal of this standard is to provide interested parties ranging from internal staff to customers and regulators with confidence that personal data is being sufficiently managed by the entity through the implementation of a personal information management system. To this end, Clause 6.15 of ISO 27701 notes that reference to this standard can be used to form the basis of a customer contract, outlining an entity's privacy-related obligations as well as the potential sanctions for noncompliance.

Certification

Organizations that meet the requirements of certifiable ISO standards can be certified by an accredited external certification body after successfully completing an audit against the standard as ISO does not provide certification or conformity assessments itself. The ISO has also issued various guidance regarding information systems generally as well as its standards, which include the following:

ISO 27701 is intended to apply to all types of organizations, irrespective of their industry, size, and nature. For example, libraries, especially large research libraries, may choose to become ISO 27701 certified (although it is not a requirement). Evidence of certification can also be used as an internal tool to assess an entity's ability to meet its own requirements related to protecting the security of information.

For example, a research library using evidence of ISO 27701 certification as a tool can demonstrate its commitment to protecting the security of information and continuously improving its security practices, which can help it to build trust with stakeholders, including employees, researchers, and funding agencies, by showing evidence of audits, commitment to security practices, controls and risk management and identification, and continuous performance monitoring.

Importantly, ISO 27701 applies to both data controllers and data processors of personal data who are required to formulate a personal information management system and who are thereby considered to be responsible and accountable for the processing of personal data. Importantly, it also takes into account the various well-known requirements of standards and legislation such as the GDPR and emphasizes the importance of mapping data management practices to these standards.

Structure of ISO 27701

ISO 27701 is structured into eight clauses that provide guidance to organizations on implementing controls within six annexes. The controls in the annexes are also considered to be relevant by default, and any deviations must be justified by organizations, typically, through evidence of a risk assessment or exemption from applicable legislation.

What follows are some of the most important clauses and annexes:

- Clause 5 outlines personal information management system requirements related to ISO 27001, while Clause 6 outlines personal information management system requirements for ISO 27002. Annex F then shows how ISO 27701 can be applied by organizations to these standards and clarifies that the ISO 27701 framework extends the information security requirements of ISO 27001 and ISO 27002 to include the protection of privacy.

- Clause 7 offers personal information management system guidance for personal data *controllers, which is supplemented by Annex A, which contains specific controls and* objectives for controllers. Clause 8 provides personal information management system guidance for personally identifiable information processors, and Annex B contains specific controls and objectives for processors.

- Annexes A and B of ISO 27701 describe requirements and guidance for either controllers or processors, with the specific objectives broken down further into controls related to conditions for collection and processing of personal data, obligations to data subjects, Privacy by Design and default, and sharing, transfer, and disclosure.

- Annex C provides information on how specific controls of ISO 27701 relate to the privacy principles of ISO 29100, while Annex E does the same for ISO 27018 and ISO 29151. Annex D informs organizations which subclauses of ISO 27701 correspond to specific articles of the GDPR, highlighting the strong links between the two regulations. However, it is important to note that ISO 27701 does not provide certification under Article 42 of the GDPR.[3]

---

[3] Article 42 of the GDPR sets out the conditions for the certification of data protection officers and the accreditation of certification bodies. It establishes a voluntary certification mechanism that aims to help organizations demonstrate their compliance with the GDPR. It is important to note that ISO 27701 does not provide certification under Article 42 of the GDPR.

Key Definitions and Basic Concepts

Some of the key definitions of ISO 27701 include:

- *Joint personally identifiable information controller*: This is generally defined as a controller of personal data that determines the purposes and means of the processing of personally identifiable information joint with one or more personally identifiable information controllers.
- *Privacy information management system*: Information security management system which addresses the protection of privacy as potentially affected by the processing of personally identifiable information.
- *Interested party/stakeholder*: Person or entity that can affect, be affected by, or perceive itself to be affected by a decision or activity.
- *Management system*: Set of interrelated or interacting elements of an organization to establish policies and objectives and processes to achieve those objectives.
- *Customer*: Depending on the role of the organization, a "customer" can be understood as either:
  - An organization in a contract with a personally identifiable information controller.
  - A personally identifiable information controller in a contract with a personally identifiable information processor.
  - A personally identifiable information processor in a contract with a subcontractor for personally identifiable information processing.

Data Processing

The requirements ISO 27701 outline various requirements related to policies, objectives, risk assessment, treatment, and monitoring and review of required for a personal information management system. Clause 5 also emphasizes the importance of senior management commitment, the involvement of employees, and the need for continual improvement of the PIMS. In addition to these general standards, organizations seeking to achieve ISO 27701 compliance must consider various factors, such as organization context, governance, policies and procedures, contractual obligations, and relevant legislation, which may impact that system.

In addition, for each type or act of processing, organizations subject to ISO 27701 must determine whether they are processing personally identifiable information as a controller, joint controller, or processor. Where more than one role applies, the entity must establish separate role-specific sets of controls. And, finally, organizations must include requirements related to the processing of personal within the scope of their personal information management system.

Retention

Once a retention schedule has been formulated, organizations should have a procedure in place to delete or deidentify logged information that contains personal data (Clause 6.9.4.2 of ISO 27701). It is also important for organizations to ensure that personal data is not stored for longer than necessary and that retention periods are clearly documented in retention schedules (Clause 7.4.7 of ISO 27701). When personal data is no longer needed, organizations should dispose of it safely according to the established procedures that consider the nature of the data (Clause 7.4.8 of ISO 27701).

Requirements Related to the Processing and Collection of Personal Data

- Clause 7.2 and Controls A.7.2 of ISO 27701 provide guidelines for processing personal data lawfully and for specific purposes. To comply with these requirements, personally identifiable information controllers must determine and document the specific purposes, lawful basis, consent process, joint controller agreements, conduct privacy impact assessments, have contracts with personally identifiable information processors, and also maintain records of personal data processing.

- Clause 8.2 and Control B.8.2 provide guidance on ensuring that personally identifiable information (PII) processors process personal data lawfully. PII processors must also keep records of their processing activities. Control B.8.2 also covers PII processor requirements for customer agreements, clarifying purposes, marketing and advertising, complying with customer instructions, and customer obligations.

ISO 27701 Management System Requirements

The information security management system requirements of ISO 27701 add to those of ISO 27001, which, generally, require organizations to:

- Conduct risk assessments at regular intervals, or whenever significant changes occur in the organization or their information systems.
- Document the risk assessment process in a manner that identifies the methodology and criteria used.
- Ensure that the assessment encompasses all data on the information assets and processing facilities including hardware, software, people, and processes.
- Evaluate risks based on their likelihood and impact, and consider potential harms including damage to confidentiality, integrity, and availability of information.
- Institute appropriate controls to mitigate risks.
- Review the risk assessment regularly to ensure effectiveness and relevance.
- Ensure management support of the risk assessment program.

In addition to the requirements of ISO 27001, ISO 27701 also requires organizations to perform information security risk assessments in compliance with ISO 27001 to identify risks related to confidentiality, integrity, and availability, as well as privacy risk assessments to identify potential privacy risks. These assessments should be followed by an evaluation of the potential impact of such events, in addition to the requirements specified in ISO 27001 (Clause 5.4.1.2).

Organizations are required under ISO 27701 to conduct privacy impact assessments as necessary, especially when planning to initiate or modify processing activities involving personal data. Such assessments may be necessary for activities such as automated decision making, large-scale processing of sensitive data, or systematic monitoring of publicly available data (as specified in Clause 7.2.5 and Control A.7.2.5 of ISO 27701).

Management of Information Security Risks

ISO 27701 mandates that organizations under its scope must assess the effect of identified risks on personal data processing and the concerned data subjects. Based on this assessment, they should prepare a Statement of Applicability outlining which controls from Annex A would be implemented or not, along with the reasons for each decision (as per Clause 5.4.1.3 of ISO 27701).

These controls include:

- Documenting a justification for each decision on whether or not to implement each control
- Describing any additional controls implemented to address privacy risks
- Outlining the entity's justification for including or excluding additional controls
- Summarizing the current status of each control, whether it has been implemented or not, and any describing planned actions to address controls that have not been implemented

Information Security Policies

According to ISO 27701, the information security policies and their review requirements of ISO 27002 are expanded to apply to the protection of information security and privacy. Additionally, organizations must establish a statement with partners, subcontractors, and any third parties, outlining their support and commitment to comply with relevant data protection laws, with clear definitions of related responsibilities (Clause 6.2.1.1 of ISO 27701).

An example of this type of statement could be:

> The organization and its partners, subcontractors, and any third parties commit to compliance with relevant data protection legislation, including GDPR. To ensure compliance, each party shall clearly define its responsibilities regarding the processing of personal data and agree to cooperate with the others to protect the confidentiality, integrity, and availability of such data. Each party shall appoint a data protection officer (DPO), ensure that their personnel are aware of and trained in data protection, and maintain appropriate technical and organizational measures to protect personal data.

Roles and Responsibilities

ISO 27701 expands the applicability of ISO 27002's security requirements which detail various elements of information security compliance, including the compliant management of information security, the handling of information assets, and the protection of information through the implementation of security controls. Topics addressed in ISO 27002 include access controls, cryptography, physical security, network security, incident management, and business continuity management. ISO 27002 also emphasizes the importance of risk assessment and management for organizations, as well as the need for ongoing monitoring, review, and improvement of information security management.

ISO 27701 extends ISO 27002's information security requirements and review to address the protection of both information security and privacy.

Additionally, ISO 27701 requires organizations to document the terms and conditions for the joint processing of personal data in a binding agreement, thereby clarifying their specific roles and responsibilities. This agreement should cover topics such as the purposes of the joint processing, the identities of the parties involved, and how the parties will ensure that data subject rights are respected. Additionally, organizations should appoint a point of contact for customers and responsible persons, known as DPOs, in some jurisdictions.

Responsible Persons (DPOs, etc.)

Under ISO 27701, an organization needs to appoint a (DPO if they are a public authority or body (except for courts acting in their judicial capacity) and their core activities consist of processing that requires the regular and systematic monitoring of data subjects on a large scale or of processing special categories of data (i.e., sensitive personal data) or data relating to criminal convictions and offenses on a large scale. This means, for example, that a body that processes sensitive data, such as health information or political affiliations, on a large scale as part of its research activities, could potentially be required to appoint a DPO. Also, even if not required by ISO 27701, organizations, including libraries, may choose to appoint a DPO voluntarily to help promote compliance with data protection laws and regulations.

Clause 6.3.1 of ISO 27701 specifies the requirements for appointing a DPO or a person in charge of data protection (PiCDP) within an organization. These include:

- Informing and advising the organization and its employees of their data protection compliance (e.g., the GDPR)
- Monitoring compliance with data protection laws and regulations and drafting and updating the organization's data protection policies and procedures
- Providing advice and guidance on data protection impact assessments (DPIAs)
- Cooperating with supervisory authorities and serving as the point of contact for data protection inquiries
- Conducting data protection training for employees and third-party data processors
- Ensuring that data protection policies and procedures are up-to-date and in compliance with relevant regulations

Additionally, a DPO/PiCDP must be appointed based on their professional qualifications, expertise, and ability to carry out their responsibilities and provided with sufficient resources and independence to perform their duties effectively.

Employment

ISO 27701 states that the information security requirements of ISO 27002 regarding screening, disciplinary procedures, and change of employment are extended to apply to the protection of information security and privacy. The overall purpose of these controls is to lower the risk of malicious or accidental actions by employees that could compromise the security of personal data. Specific requirements include:

- Screening and background checks on all new employees, contractors, and third-party users with access to personal data, which should include a verification of references, criminal records, and education and other relevant checks, depending on the sensitivity of the data being accessed, followed by documentation of such checks.
- A clear and documented disciplinary process that describes the consequences of violating information security policies and procedures is communicated to all employees and includes specific consequences for repeat offenses or particularly egregious violations.
- Immediate revocation of access to personal data when employees leave the organization, which includes revoking their access to physical and electronic systems and data and data stored on third-party systems, a mandate that all such persons should return all organizational assets, including laptops, mobile devices, and other equipment, and a requirement that any personal data stored on these devices is securely erased.

Clause 6.4 of ISO 27701 also outlines the requirements for organizations to implement procedures for managing privacy-related incidents. These requirements include:

- Having a documented incident response plan that describes the procedures required to be followed in the event of a privacy-related incident

- Complying with reporting requirements for privacy-related incidents that include reporting the incident to the relevant authorities and affected data subjects, as well as the organization's management and DPO
- Instituting specific procedures governing the investigation and assessment of data incidents, including identifying the cause, scope, and impact of the incident
- Enacting mitigation measures to lower the impact of data incidents and to prevent similar incidents from occurring in the future
- Keeping records of all privacy-related incidents, including the actions taken to redress them
- Regularly evaluating the effectiveness of the incident response plan and procedures and making necessary improvements to ensure that they remain effective and up-to-date

Awareness and Training

According to Clause 5.5 of ISO 27701, organizations seeking to comply with ISO 27701 should apply the information security principles of ISO 27001 regarding support to their personal information management system with additional resources, communication, and awareness of employees to the protection of personal data. These principles include:

- *Confidentiality*: The duty to protect personal information from unauthorized disclosure.
- *Integrity*: The obligation to ensure the accuracy and completeness of personal information processed.
- *Availability*: The requirement that organizations ensure that personal information is accessible when needed.
- *Authentication*: The obligation to verify the identity of individuals who access personal information.
- *Authorization*: Ensure that individuals have the necessary permissions to access personal information.
- *Accountability*: The creation of systems, policies, and procedures to hold relevant persons accountable for protecting personal information.

- *Nonrepudiation*: Ensuring that actions related to personal information cannot be denied. For example, through the use of an electronic signature that provides a record that can be used as evidence to prove that the person agreed to the action or transaction.
- *Compliance*: Monitoring and ensuring legal, regulatory, and contractual obligations related to personal information.
- *Risk management*: Identifying and managing risks to personal information.
- *Continual improvement*: Continually improving the effectiveness of the entity's personal information management system.

In addition to the requirements of ISO 27002, Clause 6.4.2.2 of ISO 27701 requires that organizations must implement measures to ensure that employees are aware of the impact of data breaches and policy breaches for themselves and for the data subjects, for example, through training, awareness programs, and regular reminders. And Clause 6.5.2.2 of ISO 27701 requires organizations to ensure that employees can correctly identify personal data.

In the context of a research library, these measures could include training sessions to all staff members on how to identify and report a data breach or policy violation, as well as regular reminders of the importance of safeguarding personal information provided by library patrons. Additionally, the library could create an incident response team to manage and determine the validity of reported incidents and to create a methodology for increasing the likelihood that necessary remedial actions are promptly taken.

Asset Management

Clause 6.4 of ISO 27701 states that the information security requirements of ISO 27002 regarding the management of assets extend to the protection of information security and privacy. This includes a requirement to identify the type of personal data processed, its location, the data subject's rights associated with that data, and the various risks associated with processing that data. The organization must also ensure that the data is adequately protected against unauthorized access, use, disclosure, modification, destruction, or accidental loss.

Clause 6.5.2 of ISO 27701 further requires organizations to implement an information classification system which explicitly considers how and where personal data is processed, stored, and transferred. For a research library, this type of classification system can help ensure the proper handling and protection of personal data collected from library users, such as their names, contact information, and borrowing history. For example, the library can classify personal data of its patrons and researchers based on its sensitivity, the level of risk associated with its processing, and the applicable legal requirements. The library staff can then apply appropriate security controls based on these classifications (and document those controls), such as access controls and encryption, to the personal data based on its classification. And, finally, the library can institute access controls that help to ensure that personal data is only stored and transferred to authorized recipients and in a manner that complies with applicable data protection laws and regulations.

Information Backups

Clause 6.9.3 of ISO 27701 requires organizations to create a policy that covers their requirements for the backup, recovery, restoration, and erasure of personal data as required by ISO 27002, for data, generally. These requirements include (without limitation) regularly backing up personal data based on criticality, storing personal data securely offsite to protect against data loss due to loss or disaster, encryption of backup data, testing the integrity and completeness of personal data backups (and also to ensure confidentiality), regularly testing data restoration measures, and securely erasing personal data when no longer required.

Privacy Risk Assessments

ISO 27701 requires organizations to conduct privacy risk assessments and/or privacy impact assessments to incorporate the outcomes into a Privacy by Design approach. Moreover, when conducting data testing, in cases where fake personal data cannot be used, organizations should carry out risk assessments to identify and deploy the level of suitable control for managing and mitigating related privacy risks.

A use case for a research library: For example, if the library is facilitating research that involves collecting personal data from research subjects, such as names, addresses, and contact information, a privacy risk assessment could help library management to identify potential risks to the privacy of the research subjects and determine appropriate controls to mitigate those risks. These measures can include technical safeguards such as encryption or access controls that are supplemented by organizational measures such as training staff on proper data handling procedures, drafting and updating policies and procedures, and verifying that consent is obtained from research subjects before their data is collected.

Continuous Improvement

ISO 27001 requires organizations to establish, implement, maintain, and continually improve an information security management system that promotes the confidentiality, integrity, and availability of information. This analysis should include the performance evaluation, internal auditing, and management review.

The analysis should be supplemented by an auditing process that requires organizations to conduct regular and systematic audits of their information security management system to ensure that the system is operating as intended and to continually identify areas for improvement. Further, senior management should review this system at regular intervals so as to ensure its continued suitability, adequacy, and effectiveness.

These requirements apply to the protection of personal data as per Clause 5.7 of ISO 27701. Specifically, this clause requires organizations to establish, implement, maintain, and continually improve a personal information management system that is designed to protect personal data. The performance evaluation, internal auditing, and management review processes should be applied to the personal information management system to verify that it is operating effectively and efficiently to protect personal data including the controls used to personal data protection, regular audits of the personal information management system, and reviewing the system at regular intervals to ensure its continued suitability, relevance, and effectiveness.

In the context of library management, the library can use the results of a performance evaluation, internal auditing, and management review to ensure that its personal data management system for checking out materials is effectively protecting the privacy of the data subjects. The library can then use this analysis to identify and diagnose any weaknesses or gaps in its current system and take corrective actions to address them.

Mobile Devices and Remote Work

Clause 6.3.2 of ISO 27701 requires organizations to implement appropriate measures to ensure that personal data is not at risk when accessed or processed on mobile devices or when employees are working remotely. Compliance with this requirement can include measures such as implementing access controls, mandating the use of encryption and secure connections such as VPNs, and ensuring that data is not stored locally on mobile devices.

In the context of a library, this could mean requiring employees that work remotely or who access personal data on mobile devices to use secure connections and encryption technologies when accessing the library's systems or databases. The library could also implement policies requiring that data is not stored locally on mobile devices, and access controls that provide access to personal data is restricted based on the employee's role and level of authorization. The library could also conduct risk assessments to identify potential vulnerabilities and implement appropriate controls to mitigate those risks, such as requiring the use of secure VPN connections or multifactor authentication.

Encryption

Clause 6.5.3 of ISO 27701 requires organizations, including libraries that process personal data, to document their use of removable devices like USBs. These devices can be a risk since they can leave the library's premises. As a measure to mitigate this risk, a library could verify that removable devices capable of encrypting personal data are used whenever possible. Also, the library must document any personal data from removable devices that are disposed of or physically transferred. And to prevent unauthorized access, the library must implement secure disposal procedures for the former and an authorization procedure for the latter.

Access Controls

Clause 6.6 of ISO 27701 stipulates that the access control requirements of ISO 27002 must also consider the protection of information security and privacy. These requirements include:

- Limiting personal data access to personal data to authorized individuals and preventing their unauthorized access, alteration, or destruction.
- Instituting and maintaining personal data access rights controls for employees, contractors, and third parties to personal data.
- Using multifactor authentication or other forms of best-practices authentication for accessing personal data and regularly reviewing such access controls and audit logs to identify and redress any unauthorized access attempts.
- Having updated procedures that enable the entity to manage access requests and access rights changes and to revoke access rights when an employee leaves the organization or changes roles.
- Ensuring that access to personal data is only granted on a need-to-know basis.
- Establishing controls to prevent the accidental disclosure of personal data via tools such as screen filters or password-protected screensavers.
- Establishing procedures for granting temporary access to personal data to individuals outside of the organization, such as auditors or regulators.

In addition, ISO 27701 indicates specific requirements regarding registration and deregistration to ensure the protection of personal data.

For example, organizations must ensure that registration and deregistration processes for system administrators or operators should cover procedure for potential compromise of access control. Also, Clause 6.2.2 of ISO 27701 mandates that deactivated or expired user accounts should not be reused, customer responsibilities for the protection of their user ID should be outlined, and, where applicable, checks of unused authentication credentials should be conducted as frequently as necessary.

Clause 6.2.2 also requires organizations to maintain an accurate and up-to-date record of any individual user access profiles and of the related personal data so that the individuals, organizations, and potentially the customers, where applicable, are aware of the personal data that has or has not been processed.

Finally, organizations must implement policies, procedures, or mechanisms allowing them to meet their obligations to data subjects regarding the access to and correction of their personal data (Clause 7.3.6 and Control A.7.3.6 of ISO 27701).

In a library setting, Clause 6.6 of ISO 27701's access control requirements could be applied to the protection of personal data by limiting access to library users' personal information to authorized staff members and preventing unauthorized access, alteration, or destruction of such data. Such a system would limit the access to the personal information of library users to staff with a need-to-know and would inform staff of their obligations through procedures for managing access requests and changes to access rights and the inclusion of information regarding these procedures within staff training sessions. The library should also implement multifactor authentication or other forms of secure authentication to enable secure access to personal data, and institute procedures for revoking personal data access rights when staff members leave the organization or change roles.

The library should also enact and maintain specific registration and deregistration processes governing the conduct of system administrators or operators related to a potential compromise of access control. And the library should also maintain an accurate and up-to-date record of individual user access profiles and related personal data, so library users are aware of their personal data that has or has not been processed. Finally, the library must have policies and procedures in place to allow library users to access and correct their personal data as required by ISO 27701.

Secure Disposal or Reuse of Equipment

To ensure personal data on a device that will be reused is no longer accessible, a library should follow the guidelines outlined in Clause 6.8.2.7 of ISO 27701. One way to achieve this goal is by implementing technical measures such as data encryption and/or data wiping to erase the personal data on the device. For example, the library can use software that can securely wipe data on the device to ensure that it cannot be recovered by unauthorized persons. If erasure is impractical due to performance issues, the library must implement other technical measures, such as isolating the device from the network and applying access controls, to ensure that the personal data on the device is not accessible by unauthorized persons. The library should also document the measures taken to ensure that personal data is no longer accessible on the device, to demonstrate compliance with the requirements of Clause 6.8.2.7 of ISO 27701.

Accountability and Recordkeeping

Libraries must ensure that they maintain accurate and up-to-date records to support their requirements for processing personal data. This requires appointing an individual responsible for ensuring the accuracy of the record of processing activities, which might include the type and purposes of processing, categories of personal data and recipients involved, and relevant reports from privacy impact assessments (Clause 7.2.8 and Control A.7.2.8 of ISO 27701).

Libraries that process personally identifiable information must also record the information being processed on behalf of customers, including categories of processing, any transfers of data to third countries or international organizations, and the relevant technical and organizational measures (Clause 8.2.6 and Control B.8.2.6 of ISO 27701). They must also inform their customers of any legally binding requests for disclosure of personal data to third parties, such as law enforcement, and must reject nonlegally binding requests after consulting with the customer (Clauses 8.5.4 to 8.5.5 and Controls B.8.5.4 to B8.5.5 of ISO 27701).

Finally, these libraries must identify and record the specific purposes for which the personal data will be processed (Control A.7.2.1 of ISO 27701).

For example, a library seeking to comply with Clause 7.2.8 and Control A.7.2.8 should create a record of processing activities that includes data on information such as the types of personal data collected, the purposes for processing that data, and the categories of recipients who might receive that data. The library should also designate a staff member to be responsible for ensuring the accuracy of this record. The purpose of this documentation is to provide verification of the library's compliance with ISO 27701 requirements and to provide evidence to patrons describing how their personal data is being processed and used (transparency).

In another example, a library could maintain a record of the personal data that it processes on behalf of a university research department. This record should include information on the categories of personal data being processed, any transfers of data to third countries or international organizations, and the technical and organizational measures the library has instituted to protect that data. The library can then show the university that it is processing personal data in a compliant and secure manner and that it has undertaken appropriate measures to protect that data.

CHAPTER 36

Cross-Border Transfers of Data

The requirements in ISO 27002 and ISO 27701 related to cross-border transfers are important for libraries, especially research libraries because they address the protection of personal data when it is transferred from one country to another, which tends to be highly regulated by privacy laws, and in particular, comprehensive privacy laws like the General Data Protection Regulation (GDPR). Many research libraries, in particular, collect and process personal data from users working remotely, in many jurisdictions, including researchers, students, and faculty members. This data can often include personally identifiable information, research data, and other sensitive information such as health data or social science-related data, which can include special categories of personal data as defined within the various privacy laws applicable to the institution.

Cross-border transfers of personal data involve transferring this data to another country where different privacy and data protection laws may apply. From a privacy perspective, the primary concern is that the laws within the recipient country may not offer the same level of protection as the laws of the country where the data was collected. As a result, the transfer of personal data may be at risk of unauthorized access, use, or disclosure, which could lead to identity theft, fraud, or other harmful outcomes.

ISO 27002 and ISO 27701 provide guidance on how to protect personal data during cross-border transfers. They require organizations to implement appropriate safeguards, such as encryption, access controls, and contractual agreements with third-party service providers, to ensure that personal data is protected during these transfers. Compliance with these requirements can help libraries, especially research libraries, to maintain the confidentiality, integrity, and availability of personal data and to comply with relevant laws and regulations.

Some of the main guidance elements that concern libraries related to the cross-border transfer of data include:

- The duty to perform a risk assessment to identify the risks associated with cross-border transfers of personal data that includes identifying the types of personal data that will be transferred, the countries to which the data will be transferred, and the potential risks to the data during transfer
- The obligation to understand relevant legal requirements related to cross-border transfers of personal data by the organization and to ensure that appropriate safeguards are maintained to protect the transferred data
- The requirement to obtain appropriate consent from data subjects before transferring their personal data across borders and to ensure that they are informed about the transfer and the risks involved
- The duty to maintain appropriate technical and organizational measures to protect personal data during cross-border transfers including encryption, access controls, and secure transmission methods (especially when the personal data is transmitted over untrusted networks such as the Internet or external facilities)
- The obligation to monitor and review cross-border data transfer practices to ensure that they remain effective and compliant with applicable laws and regulations
- The duty to ensure that personal data is transferred solely to authorized individuals
- The establishment of contractual agreements with third-party service providers involved in the transfer of personal data to ensure that they comply with applicable data protection laws and regulations
- The duty to enter into confidentiality agreements with employees and contractors to ensure the protection of

personal data throughout its life cycle (and specifying the time period for privacy obligations)

- The duty to account for and record the legal basis for international data transfers and any jurisdiction-specific requirements and to take into account whether data can be transferred to the jurisdictions with or without review from supervisory authorities
- The duty to record the nature, recipient, and time of transfers or disclosures of personal data to third parties

Given next are a few use cases illustrating the aforementioned principles.

A research library in the Mexico has collected personal data from its users, including researchers and students. The library wants to transfer this data to a research partner located in the European Union for a joint research project. In this case, the library would need to ensure that it complies with the EU's GDPR, which requires organizations to implement appropriate safeguards for cross-border transfers of personal data. To comply, the library would need to conduct a risk assessment, obtain appropriate consents from data subjects, and implement appropriate technical and organizational measures to protect the personal data during transfer.

A research library in Canada seeks to collaborate with a research partner located in Australia to perform a study that involves the processing and transfer of personal data. The library wants to transfer personal data, including research data and personally identifiable information, to the research partner. Here, the library would need to comply with Canada's Personal Information Protection and Electronic Documents Act (PIPEDA), which requires organizations to obtain the appropriate consent from data subjects before transferring their personal data outside of Canada. The library would also need to obtain the consent of the data subjects and ensure that the personal data is protected during the transfer.

A research library in Germany wants to collect personal data from its users, including researchers and students. It also wants to transfer this data to a cloud-based data storage provider located in the United States for storage and analysis. In this case, the library would need to comply with the EU's GDPR, local German data protection standards and interpretations, and also with the US Cloud Act, which provides that communication service providers must comply with legal requests for data from the U.S. government, "regardless of whether such communication, record, or other information is located within or outside of the United States." The library would also need to implement appropriate technical and organizational measures such as encryption and similar technologies to protect the personal data during the transfer and ensure that the cloud provider complies with both the GDPR and the Cloud Act.

CHAPTER 37

Vendor Management Issues

ISO 27701 outlines several requirements that organizations must follow when using third-party service providers to store or back up personal data, transfer physical media, or process personal data on behalf of a customer. For instance, organizations subject to ISO 27701 must use appropriate controls when choosing third-party service providers for personal data storage or backup (Clause 6.9.3). They must also define roles for event log reviews and address any access to logs between multiple service providers (Clause 6.9.4.1). Supplier agreements must also stipulate all relevant roles and responsibilities for any third parties, taking into account the categories of personal data being processed and the mechanism the organization will use to manage compliance (Clause 6.12.1.2).

In the context of research libraries, these principles could be applied when working with third-party vendors to digitize and store collections. For example, a research library using a third-party vendor to digitize rare manuscripts and store them in the cloud must ensure that it uses appropriate controls to safeguard the personal data contained in the manuscripts. The library must also clearly define roles for event log reviews, address any access to logs between multiple service providers, and ensure that the supplier agreement allocates all relevant roles and responsibilities of any third parties.

Organizations subject to ISO 27701 must also apply the principles of Privacy by Design and Privacy by Default to any outsourced information systems whenever possible (Clause 6.11.2.7). And contracts that are entered into with processors of personal data must require parties processing personal data to comply with the selected controls from Annex B of ISO 27701 (Clause 7.2.6).

When organizations process personal data on behalf of a customer, processing must be limited to the purposes stated in the customer's (the data controller's) documented instructions, which stipulate among other types of information, the goals, controls, security measures, and deadlines for the completion of the required services (Clause 8.2.2). Customers such as end-users should be notified of any contract infringements and violations of instructions related to the processing of personal data, and organizations must be able to demonstrate compliance with customer instructions (Clauses 8.2.4 to 8.2.5).

With respect to research libraries, this principle could be applied when a library works with a third-party vendor to manage library cardholder data. The third-party vendor, seeking to comply with ISO 27701, must process the data in accordance with the library's documented instructions (the library is the controller) and must also comply with various contractual goals, controls, security measures, and deadlines, for example, the duty to notify the other party of any infringements of the contract and instructions regarding processing of personal data.

Processors of personal data must obtain written authorization from customers prior to any change of subcontractor that acts as a data processor and must inform the customer of any cross-border data transfers to third parties in enough time to allow the customer to reject them if necessary (Clauses 8.5.1 and 8.5.8).

For example, a vendor that works with a library to manage library e-mail communications must receive written authorization from the library prior to any change of subcontractor and must also inform the library of any cross-border data transfers to third parties with enough time so as to allow the library to possibly reject the appointment.

In addition to the requirements of ISO 27002 and jurisdiction-specific privacy regulations, organizations must clarify responsibilities and procedures for the prevention, identification, notification to relevant parties or authorities, and documentation of any data breaches or security incidents. The record should contain sufficient information, for example, pertaining to the description, consequences, timeframe, and management of the incident, as would enable the provision of a report. For personally identifiable information processors, the breach notification procedure should be clarified within the contract between the customer and organization (Clause 6.13 of ISO 27701).

ISO 27701 highlights that a security event involving personal data does not necessarily necessitate a review.

Organizations are required to implement a process to constantly review event logs to determine any issues. The process must include continuous, automated, or manual monitoring and notifying of processes (Clause 6.9.4.1 of ISO 27701).

CHAPTER 38

Information Governance— An OECD Perspective[1]

Why Do Government Entities Need To Be Concerned About Information Governance?

A May 2017 article from *The Economist* coined the term "data is the new oil."[2] While the general premise of this article was to increase public awareness regarding the dangers of consolidated power among the tech giants, the term also helped to raise public awareness of the importance of data as an important asset that, if managed wisely, can yield tremendous benefits to both private industry and to the public sphere.

Over the past decades, numerous governments and government entities have increased their creation and implementation of policies and guidelines aimed at addressing data governance within their organizational units, albeit at a slower pace than entities in the private sphere. This section discusses some of these efforts and also presents several proposed models for public sector data governance, derived primarily from OECD good practices on public sector data management and governance, as outlined by the OECD.[3]

From a governmental perspective, important purposes of good data governance include establishing a common vision; enhancing coherent implementation and coordination; and strengthening the institutional,

---

[1] Id.

[2] www.economist.com/leaders/2017/05/06/the-worlds-most-valuable-resource-is-no-longer-oil-but-data.

[3] Data governance in the public sector | The Path to Becoming a Data-Driven Public Sector | OECD iLibrary (oecd-ilibrary.org).

regulatory, capacity, and technical foundations to better control and manage the data value cycle, that is, collect, generate, store, secure, process, share, and reuse data, as a means to enhance trust and deliver value.[4]

This is especially true in today's day and age as governments aim to become more data driven as part of their digital strategy. Like private sector actors, governments need to extract value from data assets; enable their stakeholders (including the public) to obtain greater data access; share and integrate at both an organizational level and beyond; and increase their overall efficiency and accountability. This is especially true given the trend by regulators to target government agencies for fines based on their breach of, for example, privacy laws.

What Are Some of the Current Trends in the Management and Sharing of Public Sector Data?[5]

The OECD has observed various trends in the governance, management, and sharing of public sector data including:

- The increasingly deep relationship between data governance and data protection practices at the global scale that is marked by the need to balance the danger of data overprotection with the benefits value of data sharing, such as in the delivery of cross-border public services.
- The growing trend of government intervention to improve the protection of personal data and the prioritization of ethical and transparent use of data by politicians and regulators.
- The recognition that data governance is no longer a matter limited to national or organizational boundaries, but a multinational concern resulting from cross-border data sharing that has been triggered by the increased data flows among organizations and sectors (e.g., business-to-government), creating additional complexity.

---

[4] Id.
[5] Id.

- The increasing awareness that data overprotection can result from the misunderstanding of national and international regulations and drive change in terms of policy approaches.
- The recognition of the need for including data governance oversight within governments' overall digital transformation policies and the need to implement holistic, cohesive, and unified policies that are marked by common but flexible data tools (e.g., data-sharing platforms) provide solutions that can be reused across the broad public sector.
- The need to ensure the proper management of data through its entire life cycle, which is closely connected to the need to strengthen public sector data leadership and stewardship within the public sector and to improve data management practices, for example, around the production, storing, processing, and sharing toward higher data openness and, eventually, to increases in productivity.
- Progress by some countries such as Canada, Ireland, the Netherlands, the United Kingdom, and the United States toward implementing overarching data strategies as a means to build greater public sector cohesion and promote the integration of policies and tools throughout the government data value cycle.

Despite these strides, throughout the OECD, governments face many of the same obstacles as private sector entities. The most important of these challenges include:

- The lack of understanding among many government entities that data governance is not the primary or, in some cases, even exclusive responsibility of IT—and of the benefits of instituting and maintaining a broader regulatory framework that accounts for and unifies variant capacities, policies, regulatory frameworks, and leadership and organizational cultures that can only be obtained through maintaining strategic public sector approaches to data governance.

- The continued focus on the resolution of technical issues as the primary goal of data governance—leading to off-mark data-related policy decisions. For example, concentrating on the creation of technological solutions such as application programming interfaces (APIs) and data standards without enabling the adequate organizational, governance, and cultural context to make those tools relevant to address policy challenges.

- The need among many OECD countries to define strategic roles (e.g., data stewards, chief data officers) to support data governance via a stronger institutional fabric. Establishing these roles is critical to scaling and sustaining policy implementation and building greater data maturity across the public sector.

- Public policies that tend to overlook the benefits of data governance. There is a need for promoting data governance as a sublayer of policy arrangements. This can help to extract value from data for successful policy.

- A continued failure by policy makers to recognize the key contribution of data governance to policy success. This is particularly relevant in the context of cross-cutting public policies that require the sharing of, and access to, data from multiple public sector entities for policy monitoring, compliance, and evaluation purposes or in the context of cross-sectoral data-sharing practices and governance arrangements (e.g., business-to-government data sharing)

The most important concept to take away is that good data governance is not the responsibility of a small group of people and that policies, procedures, and outlooks must be adapted to the current (and future) globalized, fast-paced, diverse, digital, and interconnected world. This means governments must develop open, inclusive, iterative, collective, and value-based data approaches when putting in place their data governance initiatives. To do this, governments must obtain meaningful input from a broad array of stakeholders who can then help to better identify government data policy priorities and data needs and to assess the current context in terms of data capability.

Why Is Good Data Governance Important?

The OECD cites various core institutional benefits to good data governance by governmental entities. These include:

- Assisting to establish a common institutional vision
- Allowing for the coherent implementation and multilateral coordination of policies and procedures
- Strengthening institutional, regulatory, capacity, and technical foundations so as to allow various governmental organizations to better control and manage the collection, generation, storage, security, processing, sharing, and reuse of data in a manner that delivers value to both the public and the various governmental stakeholders
- Enabling government institutions to enhance the value extracted from their data assets, which facilitates greater data access, sharing, and integration
- Enhancing public and internal stakeholder access to data, including the sharing and integration of important information assets

What Are Some of the Important Goals and Benefits of Good Data Governance?

The OECD cites a series of important goals and benefits of good governmental data governance including:

- The inclusion of data governance principles into the realm of data protection and the implementation of data governance concepts into various data privacy laws, including, most prominently, the GDPR, which has emphasized the need to

create common frameworks to ensure the safe transmission of
data across borders;

- The increased inclusion of data governance principles
  within governments' broader digital transformation policies,
  necessitating the development of holistic approaches to
  information governance (IG) and its benefits to "good
  government" as a whole. At their best, these approaches can
  yield the development of common but flexible data tools
  such as data-sharing platforms and create solutions to allow
  the reuse of data on a broad basis throughout the public
  sector, ensure the proper management of data throughout its
  entire life cycle, and yield solutions such as the development
  of data registers as a means to improve interinstitutional
  data sharing and collaboration.

- The growing awareness among policy makers that data
  governance is no longer the exclusive responsibility of IT
  departments, which, when fully realized, can lead to the
  development of broad-based strategic approaches to address
  the transformation and cohesiveness of capacities, policies,
  regulatory frameworks, and organizational culture.

- The close relationship between good data governance
  policies and public sector reforms generally, especially when
  such governance is marked by embedding various data
  governance elements within government structures, leading to
  improvements in open governance, public service leadership
  and capability, and budgetary governance.

- The expansion of data governance policy ownership from
  the control of a few isolated individuals to that of a broader
  range of stakeholders, who can, in turn, help to better identify
  data policy priorities and data needs and to assess the current
  context in terms of data capability within the public sector.
  These stakeholders can include both government bodies
  and actors outside the public sector, participating through
  partnerships, such as cloud or SaaS service providers who can
  help to create solutions that are tailored to the unique needs
  of government entities.

What Are Some of the Core Elements of a Successful Public Sector Information Governance Scheme?[6]

The OECD suggests a series of core questions for stakeholders seeking to implement a successful public sector IG scheme. These include:

- Whether the planned scheme supports the entity's business strategy, and in particular, do the relevant stakeholders have a clear idea of the expected outcomes and priorities of their IG program—for example, a program aimed at increasing efficiency is likely to have a disparate series of priorities from a program geared toward increasing ethics and values.
- As discussed earlier, in the case of the allocation of agency responsibility for IG initiatives within the context of the U.S. federal government, which entities are supporting the initiative and, in addition, which stakeholders are included within the decision-making process, and do these stakeholders have the necessary skillsets and perspectives required to successfully implement the stated initiatives?
- What skills are needed to successfully implement the stated purpose of the initiative—thoroughly targeting and assessing the skill strengths and gaps among the core IG team is critical to program success.
- How can the organization successfully standardize the data skill needs of the prospective team members so as to promote interinstitutional mobility and career development—ideally, given the common pay disparities between government institutions and the private sector, it is imperative for government institutions to retain core talent.
- How can the organization spread knowledge from learning silos toward a collective knowledge of IG principles—for example, through both digital and physical platforms, enhanced learning environments, and other efforts aimed at promoting peer-to-peer learning and knowledge sharing?

---

[6] www.oecd-ilibrary.org/sites/9cada708-en/index.html?itemId=/content/component/9cada708-en.

- How can the organization optimize its use of external talent and acknowledge through the development of open knowledge practices and the engagement with actors outside the public sector ecosystem such as universities and private sector companies?

Additional Challenges Facing Effective Government Agency IG Implementation[7]

Additional challenges facing government bodies in their quest to establish a coherent and effective IG framework include:

- The inherent conflict between the organizational need to adopt a structured approach that simultaneously allows for the flexibility required to implement tailored and scalable IG solutions. Further, the unique characteristics of each data ecosystem can create additional complications to the data governance environment as these solutions are adjusted to meet the different needs of the various stakeholders, variant organizational size, and varying levels of data maturity— factors that only proliferate with the evolution of the data governance environment.
- Complexities introduced by the sharing of data among units, departments, and bodies within the same organization— in order to manage this sharing effectively, government organizations must implement common data governance frameworks and tools, which become increasingly important as the number of outside stakeholders increases.
- The need to promote good data governance in sector-specific areas such as health data while simultaneously managing the security and privacy risks posed by the transfer of such data.
- Challenges faced by data transfers and data sharing within the context of a multilevel governance system composed of a federal government and various state or provincial governments, particularly when the balance between central

---

7 www.oecd-ilibrary.org/sites/9cada708-en/index.html?itemId=/content/
component/9cada708-en.

and local power impacts the central government's ability to access data sets owned and controlled by local authorities and where local authorities may utilize controls that differ from those of the central government.

- The necessity of increased government action and vigilance to ensure the protection and ethical use of personal data following their cross-border transfer. An additional challenge posed by this increased transfer is the need by governments to involve myriad stakeholders ranging from international organizations to private business and nongovernmental organizations. The involvement of these disparate parties heightens the need for the development of more robust international data governance arrangements and increasingly coherent multinational standards and coordination levels.

Specific Measures That Can Be Taken to Promote Effective Public Sector Information Governance[8]

A well-planned public sector IG policy should include at least the following elements:

- A common, broad-based IG policy that encourages various agencies to share information on both a central and a local government level.
- Assembly of the right team—as with the private sector, it is imperative that this team include, at the very least, representatives from IT, compliance, records management, and legal.
- Strong "corporate" support.
- Effective due diligence that highlights the risks of basing IG planning premises on faulty or insufficient information. The IG team must, in this respect, emphasize the risks posed by the types of information that could be exposed or lost and should inform senior management of the risks and consequences of

---

[8] https://governmentbusiness.co.uk/features/how-important-information-governance.

data breaches, particularly when those breaches involve sensitive personal data such as health information.

- Creation of and regularly updating IG policies and, in this vein, placing a special emphasis on those areas where the content is either highly sensitive or where governance is weakest such as in the areas of e-mail or mobile.
- Automating retention management systems and auditing these systems to ensure and verify their proper function.
- Prioritize the regulation of e-mail and, when addressing management decision makers, ensure the use of value-based criteria to establish retention policies, determine archival arrangements, and ensure that archives are optimized for e-discovery, search, and legal hold.
- Use appropriate tools to assist government agencies to delete redundant, outdated, or trivial (ROT) content. These tools can include automated metadata correction programs, deduplication, and automated retention policy enforcement measure and search capability improvement.
- Institute the technical measures required to ensure that scanned documents are searchable by recapturing them with modern optical character recognition (OCR) technologies that allow for the creation of enhanced metadata and data analytics improvements.
- Implement day-forward automated classification technologies, particularly with respect to e-mail, process archives and routine inbound content, as well as simplify user filing accuracy.

Case Studies

European Commission Case Study of Policy Initiative for Open Access to Research Data (Horizon 2020 Open Research Data (ORD) Pilot and Data Management Plan)[9]

The relevant initiative, which was overseen by the European Commission and other relevant bodies, was also known as the Horizon 2020 Open Research

---

[9] Case Study of Policy Initiative for Open Access to Research Data, European Union, 2018.

Data (ORD) Pilot and Data Management Plan (DMP), and spanned seven years, from 2014 to 2020. The formulators sought to improve and maximize access to and reuse of research data generated by Horizon 2020 projects,[10] taking into account the need to balance openness and protection of scientific information (e.g., IP rights, personal data protection). It also aimed to introduce data management as part of the research process.

Achieving these goals, the drafters believed, would move the EU member states toward policy alignment and thus toward the development of a better and more unified environment for research collaboration in European Research Area and beyond it.

Particularly concerning to the European Commission was the fact that member states had vastly variant policies and strategies for enhancing the cross-border flow and transparency of research data, as indicated in the given chart. This inequity had several potentially negative ramifications including both regulatory and trade related.

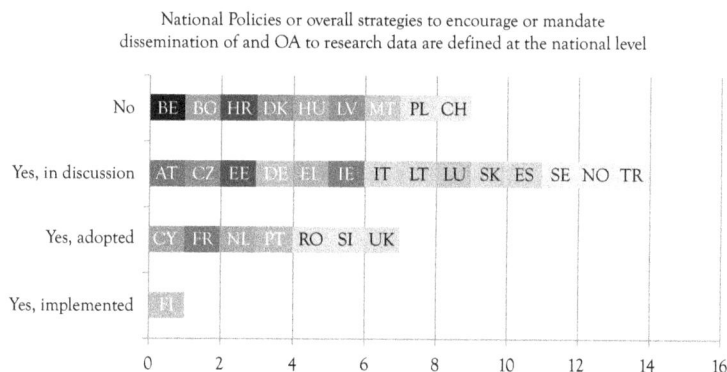

National Policies or overall strategies to encourage or mandate
dissemination of and OA to research data are defined at the national level

No	BE	BG	HR	DK	HU	LV	MT	PL	CH
Yes, in discussion	AT	CZ	EE	DE	EL	IE	IT	LT	LU	SK	ES	SE	NO	TR
Yes, adopted	CY	FR	NL	PT	RO	SI	UK
Yes, implemented	FI

0   2   4   6   8   10   12   14   16

Policies or strategies on open research data at the national level, Report on the implementation of Commission Recommendation C(2012) 4890 – Study, Commission, 2018

In addition to this inequity, member states also exhibited varying degrees of commitment to ensuring the open flow of data—and, in

---

[10] Usefully, the initiative defined open access as the practice of providing online access to scientific information that is free of charge to the user and that is reusable. In the context of R&D, and with respect to scientific information, it involves open access to peer-reviewed scientific publications and scientific research data.

particular, funders of research projects in some member states required openness and transparency as an evaluation criterion for funding, whereas other member states did not.

The operational objectives of the recommendation concerning research data were: (a) to stimulate the implementation of open access policies for data by member states that require the deposit of research data resulting from publicly funded research in an e-infrastructure and support the setup and maintenance of digital e-infrastructures; and (b) to support the setup and maintenance of digital e-infrastructures for the preservation of scientific information and promote effective deposit systems for born-digital scientific information.

The initiative sought to achieve these goals by, among other priorities, instituting various IG-centered controls and processes. These included:

- Instituting a data management plan outlining the data management life cycle for the data to be collected, processed, or generated by the research project and explain how the FAIR principles[11] are followed, and particularly, what data will be collected, processed, and/or generated; which methodology and standards will be applied; whether data will be shared or made open access; and how data will be curated and preserved (including after the end of the project).

- Creation of a detailed stakeholder consultation process, following which 72 percent of respondents stated that they totally or partially agreed that there is a need for policy intervention in open science.

- Detailed adoption guidelines including requirements to deposit research data needed to validate the results presented in scientific publications, including associated metadata, in the repository as soon as possible, to take measures to enable

---

[11] In the context of research data management, FAIR principles ensure that research outputs are findable, accessible, interoperable, and reusable. In practice, they enable higher visibility and reuse potential for data.

any third party to access, mine, exploit, reproduce, and disseminate (free of charge for any user) this research data, and to provide information via the chosen repository about the tools available for the researchers to validate the results, for example, specialized software or software code, algorithms, and analysis protocols.

- Monitoring and evaluation criteria.

Research Data Management and Openness in Slovenia, June 22, 2018[12]

The Slovenian government sought to implement a new open access strategy to promote its adoption of a new Research and Development Activity Act to promote open access to research data. The action plan for the implementation of the national open access strategy required the pilot for this plan to be defined, implemented, and analyzed, and for recommendations for the policy to be prepared. The plan aimed to cover all strategic issues suggested by OECD, that is, data governance for trust (addressing privacy, confidentiality, quality, and ethical issues), discoverability/findability, machine readability and data standards, recognition and reward system for data authors, definition of responsibility and ownership, business models for open data provision, and building human capital and institutional capabilities at public agencies, to manage, create, curate, and reuse data. The target stakeholders were the beneficiaries of scientific funding.

The plan sought to create Slovenian provisions for research data management and openness that avoided the pitfall of being designed as stand-alone solutions, but that would, instead, be fully aligned with international recommendations. In addition, by instituting a national approach to the design of provisions, the formulators sought to increase its efficiency as compared to having separate provisions governing individual research funding and research performing organizations.

---

[12] Case Study on Research Data Management and Open... |OECD.

Specific pitfalls included:

- A shortage of data experts in the country, which the formulators predicted would slow down the implementation.
- Gaps in the awareness and skills of researchers regarding research data management and openness need a lot of input.
- Additional effort required to ensure open research data in research evaluation processes would stimulate researchers to more quickly embrace openness.

Seeking to overcome these pitfalls, the Slovenian government sought to create a framework that:

- Had a broad-based approach involving input by multiple stakeholders operating at different levels of government at both a local and a national level.
- Was marked by continued executive sponsorship—political leadership was active at the level of government in both the formulation and the drafting of the plan. In addition, input was sought by the OECD and the European Commission, who were indirectly presented through their policy recommendations (and regulations in case of the European Union).
- Transparent management which was sought to be achieved, at least in part, by presenting the initiative to the Council for Science and Technology (a body counseling the Government of the Republic of Slovenia), to the Slovenian Rectors' Conference, to the Coordination of Independent Slovenian Research Institutions as well as at events for researchers and to other stakeholders.
- Reflected a broad array of data, including associated metadata.
- Was accessible—a stated goal of the project was to make research data as accessible as soon as possible.

Finally, the program sought to establish accountability systems: responsibility to reach stated targets was assigned specifically to the major research funding organization in Slovenia, that is, the Slovenian Research Agency, and supervised by the Ministry of Education, Science and Sport as the guardian of the national open access strategy and its Chapter 7 on Pilot Programme Open Access to Research Data. And finally the Ministry was charged to actively work with the agency to ensure that targets will be met.

Open Access Dissemination in the Spanish Law of Science, Technology and Innovation Initiative (Article 37)[13]

The strategic goal of the initiative was to assist researchers funded by public calls to deposit the final digital version of their contributions to journals in an open access repository. It was part of a governmental attempt at long-term digital transformation of publicly funded research overseen by the Spanish Secretary of State for Universities, Research, Development and Innovation of the Ministry of Science, Innovation and Universities, beginning in 2011.

The initiative was triggered by a broad stakeholder consensus on the benefits of open access, and, particularly, removing the legal, commercial, and technological barriers to access of scientific information and increasing transparency. In addition, the formulators believed that the open access initiative would prevent duplication, foster knowledge and technological transfer, and promote innovation.

Its main goals were to:

- Promote and coordinate the national infrastructure of open access digital scientific repositories in an interoperable manner based on the standards adopted by the global community.
- Foster, support, and facilitate the adoption of open access policies by all researchers from universities and public research organizations, the main producers of scientific knowledge in Spain.

---

[13] https://community.oecd.org/servlet/JiveServlet/downloadBody/148992-102-1-263212/Spanish%20Law%20of%20Science%2C%20Technology%20and%20Innovation%20v2.pdf.

- Create greater visibility, and both domestic and international application of the results from research carried out in Spain.

Initiative stakeholders included:

- R&D public funding agencies which draft the guidelines on open access to science and establish the terms under which these should be fulfilled
- Universities and research centers charged with applying the initiative's mandates, creating institutional practices, and maintaining the various technical infrastructures required to comply with them
- Individual who have to adopt new actions and processes to their research work
- Institutional subscribers to scientific journals, who stand to benefit open access mandates and who need to adapt to them

The main stakeholder challenge was to develop a common language and approach for managing data in accordance with the initiative. This was especially true as each group had a disparate corporate language and business culture. In response to this challenge, a working group was established to voice the experience of the various institutions, establish the steps needed to be taken, and create a more unified approach to isolating the challenges and difficulties of effectively implementing the initiative.

From a project management perspective, in 2017, the Monitoring Commission committed to overseeing progress on the initiative, including:

- Monitoring compliance with open access publishing
- Optimizing archiving
- Focusing on researchers regarding open access and new indicators
- Reducing journal costs

- Transparency in journal subscription agreements and control mechanisms

The final critical element was to ensure corporate sponsorship of the initiative at a broad governmental level. This included:

- Obtaining central government support of the open access to research data in the state plan as one of a number of key movements toward open science
- Achieving public acknowledgement of the need for developing the digital skills of predoctoral candidates in the sciences, creating the mechanism for continued adoption of the initiative's goals
- Creating a monitoring and reporting system to verify program progress that includes regular policy monitoring, the establishment of milestones, participation in the reorganization and coordination of subscription and open access models with the key resource and scientific information suppliers—publishers—at national level
- Establishment of a permanent expert review board
- A commitment to review and adopt measures for the effective promotion of open science and to monitor the calls for proposals of the state plan, including manuals, best practices and management forms, and open access to research results and data (DMP).

Mexican Open Science Policy: Open Institutional Repositories Program[14]

The purpose of this program, which commenced in 2015, was to gather, preserve, and secure open access to scientific and technological innovation, mainly public-funded information resources, including databases.

---

[14] https://community.oecd.org/servlet/JiveServlet/downloadBody/149104-102-2-263395/Mexico.pdf.

Similar to the Slovenian and Spanish models, the Mexican program sought to increase open data sharing among both the scientific community and the general public. It also sought to develop institutional data repositories developed and interconnected with the National Repository and institutional capacities for research data management developed under the Open Repositories Program and make thousands of data sets open access available within the National Repository.

Also, the main rationale for this initiative is to bolster the National Open Science Policy and to retrieve as many data sets as possible. Central goals of the project include bringing Mexican standards of openness in line with best-practice international standards for both open and national data repositories and increasing opportunities for involvement among the academic community.

As with many developing countries, political stability was cited as a primary potential obstacle, underscoring the role of continued corporate sponsorship in promoting project success.

From an IG perspective, the program was less centralized than either the Spanish or the Slovenian program and, specifically:

- Relegated the duty to design governance models for trust, privacy, confidentiality, quality, and ethical issues to each institution on an individual basis
- Used the OpenAIRE metadata[15] for data standard
- Assigned principal compliance responsibility to the participating institutions—not the National Repository
- Established means for stakeholder development, such as seminars and workshops, emphasizing that while some efforts have been made to develop capacities like seminars and workshops, all of these efforts are designed for open repositories managers.

---

[15] OpenAIRE is a European project supporting the Open Science movement. It allows for a network of dedicated Open Science experts to promote and provide training on Open Science fundamentals. It also serves as a technical infrastructure that gathers research findings from connected data providers (What is OpenAIRE and How Does it Make Science More Open? (orvium.io)).

According to the OECD report, the main achievements included:

- Developing a single technical framework (OpenAIRE) for open research data management within the country
- Creating more than 10 data repositories projects ongoing and over 27,000 research data sets.
- Developing the repositories' national experts' community working and fostering the development of international efforts like Microsoft DataVerse.

CHAPTER 39

The U.K. Government Information Principles

In 2011, the U.K. government published a series of seven core information governance principles, which can be summarized as follows:[1]

1. *Principle 1—Recognition of Information as a Valued Asset*
   - Government organizations must:
     - Create a framework that emphasizes the importance of data assets as a business asset.
     - Continually refine their approach toward handling these assets by identifying, categorizing and cataloging both information assets, themselves, and their usage among the various organizational units.
     - Quantify and regularly assess and record the value of information assets.
2. *Principle 2—Management of Information*
   - Government organizations must:
     - Establish a framework for managing information throughout its various life cycle stages.
     - Continually define their approach to digital continuity and their risk, assessment, and risk management framework.
     - Develop a coherent approach toward ensuring legal and regulatory compliance and information governance standards.
     - Create and enhance a skills development framework or maturity model that develops organizational capabilities and that fosters an information management culture.

---

[1] https://assets.publishing.service.gov.uk/government/uploads/system/uploads/attachment_data/file/266286/Information_Principles_UK_Public_Sector_final.odt.

3. *Principle 3—Ensuring That Information Is Fit for Its Purpose*
   o Government organizations must:
     - Define their approach to managing information that determines the required quality of information that is necessary to meet the purpose for which it is collected or maintained.
     - Create consistent modalities for describing, recording, and communicating information quality and processes and governance standards for continually monitoring that quality.
     - Ensure that the technology platforms they use support their quality goals.

4. *Principle 4—Information Is Standardized and Linkable*
   o Government organizations must:
     - Commit to establishing open standards that are transparent and publicly available.
     - Establish frameworks for corporate standards and for linking information.
     - Create a pragmatic framework for migrating to standardized, linkable data.

5. *Principle 5—Reuse of Information*
   o Government organizations must:
     - Foster opportunities to effectively and proactively reuse data.
     - Create mechanism for understanding and, where possible, overcoming obstacles to the reuse of data.
     - Establish approaches for promoting and discovering which data can be reused.
     - Develop a coherent approach to managing reference or master data.

6. *Principle 6—Publication of Information*
   o Government institutions must:
     - Institute a framework for responding to legal obligations regarding public information access.
     - Proactively categorize information that they maintain to filter out data that is irrelevant or unsuitable for publication.

- Create channels and processes for publishing information.
- Develop a pragmatic migration approach for publishing data.

7. *Principle 7—Public Access to Information*
   o Government organizations must:
   - Institute and maintain a framework for responding to their legal obligations regarding citizens' access to information and the rights of citizens to know how their data has been used.
   - Create systems that go beyond their legal obligations and to identify opportunities to proactively make information about citizens available to them by default.
   - Establish coherent approaches to discovering personal information.
   - Develop a pragmatic migration approach that enables citizens to access their information.

An updated version of these principles, published in May 2020,[2] builds upon initiatives such as the Industrial Strategy, the AI Review, the AI Sector Deal, and the Research and Development Roadmap—setting out a framework for how the U.K. government intends to approach and invest in data to strengthen its economy. The principles outlined four basic priorities underpinning the U.K. government's National Data Strategy, namely:

1. *Data foundations*: The true value of data can only be fully realized when it is fit for purpose; recorded in standardized formats on modern, future-proof systems; and held in a condition that means it is findable, accessible, interoperable, and reusable. By improving the quality of the data, we can use it more effectively and drive better insights and outcomes from its use.
2. *Data skills*: To make the best use of data, we must have a wealth of data skills to draw on. That means not only delivering the right skills through our education system, but also ensuring that people can continue to develop the data skills they need throughout their lives.

---

[2] National Data Strategy – GOV.UK (www.gov.uk).

3. *Data availability*: For data to have the most effective impact, it needs to be appropriately accessible, mobile, and reusable. That means encouraging better coordination; access to and sharing of data of appropriate quality between organizations in the public, private, and third sectors; and ensuring appropriate protections for the flow of data internationally.

4. *Responsible data*: As we drive increased use of data, we must ensure that it is used responsibly, in a way that is lawful, secure, fair, ethical, sustainable, and accountable, while also supporting innovation and research.

The U.K. National Data Strategy[3]

Published in May 2022, the 2022 U.K. National Data Strategy sets out the government's ambitions to improve data use in government and the importance of sharing data to deliver better services and outcomes for businesses and people.

Generally, the framework applies to a wide array of professionals including:

- Senior leaders who are responsible for setting the strategy and direction for a government organization or department
- Persons who work in the digital data and technology professions or knowledge and information management professions in data-related roles as data-sharing practitioners
- Persons who work in a role that focuses on data provision or data acquisition as data requester
- Persons who regularly or occasionally need to access data from other parts of government, but are not as specialized as a data-sharing practitioner

Also, the framework applies to the U.K. government departments (not including councils) agencies of the U.K. government departments,[4] and local governments are not bound by its principles.

---

[3] Data Sharing Governance Framework – GOV.UK (www.gov.uk).

[4] The Northern Ireland Executive, Scottish Government, and Welsh Government have their own approaches to data-sharing governance and are not bound by the framework.

Further, the local government is not required to implement these principles and actions.

The purpose of the framework is to provide best-practice principles and actions to reduce or remove common nontechnical frictions and barriers, both currently and in the future, which the drafters believe will set departments and public bodies on a course to greater alignment of data-sharing systems and processes, and embed data sharing as a strategic priority across government. It also supports commitments made in:

- The U.K. National Data Strategy,[5] including addressing barriers to data sharing and driving aligned data governance structures across government
- The Declaration on Government Reform,[6] which commits to openness and data sharing across government

The drafters of the framework acknowledged both the technical challenges posed by legacy systems and embedding of consistent data standards as well as various nontechnical barriers to sharing data in the public sector—and the strategy seeks to overcome these obstacles. In addition, many of the specific barriers to implementing an efficient information governance plan closely mirror those faced by private sector actors. These include:

- Public sector bodies that have not set data sharing as a strategic priority.
- A lack of alignment between organizations in data-sharing systems and processes and when we have different approaches to navigating the complexities of legal and ethical compliance.
- Evolving data protection and ethical issues.
- The recognition that while data is essential to delivering good public services, developing and evaluating policy, and a wide range of government operations, the data needed to do this

---

[5] www.gov.uk/government/publications/uk-national-data-strategy/national-data-strategy.

[6] www.gov.uk/government/publications/declaration-on-government-reform.

well is often held in different parts of government and needs
to be shared so that it can be used.

- Challenges posed by the dearth of clear and common
technical standards, which are fundamental to the way data is
represented, recorded, described, stored, shared, and accessed;
clear and common governance standards are needed to deliver
data to the right place at the right time.

- Issues related to data siloing, different levels of data maturity, and
solving problems in isolation have contributed to inconsistencies
and misalignment in our data-sharing governance.

In an effort to meet these challenges, the framework outlined five
principles aimed at increasing the efficiency of data sharing by government agencies, which bear a close resemblance to the classic underpin-
nings of information governance support[7]:

1. *Commit to leadership and accountability for data sharing:*
   o On a practical level, this means ensuring that government
      organizations should:
      - Have enough information to make strategic decisions and
         deliver high-quality services and to assist other people in
         government to do the same.
      - Make data sharing a strategic priority, which, in practical
         terms, requires organizations to make sure that the use
         and reuse of data, including accessing data from other
         government organizations is accessible.
      - Create a culture that supports people working to solve
         data-sharing problems (monitoring and accountability).
2. *Make it easy to start data sharing:*
   o This means that government organizations should ensure
      that it is easy for others to contact them about accessing
      their data—including by, for example, establishing a single
      point of contact to triage requests and queries.

---

[7] And, in particular, the concepts of transparency, corporate program support
and awareness.

3. *Maximize the value of the data held*:
   - On a practical level, this means:
     - Ensuring that the organization records what data it holds and who is its responsible owner, that is, who is responsible for the data and what data is held (an inventory)—a lack of accountability can lead to potentially valuable data not being reused, or being shared inappropriately.
     - Ensuring that people can discover what data is held by the organization—by, for example, creating a data catalog or data asset inventory or contributing to an existing one, as well as a data asset register that complies with the Data Protection Act 2018.

4. *Support responsible data sharing*:
   - On a practical level, this means ensuring the presence of transparent data sharing practices such as:
     - Consulting with data protection professionals as soon as the organization starts to consider data sharing or accessing or acquiring personal data.
     - Making it easy for users who want to access the organization's data to identify the laws which allow it to share data (including, without limitation, the U.K. GDPR for sharing personal data)—when government departments and public bodies share data with each other they must identify a legal power for sharing personal data.
     - Making it easy to collaborate on data protection impact assessments (DPIAs)[8] and sharing agreements.
     - Ensuring that users of the organization's data can access important information about existing DPIAs and sharing agreements—and, particularly, making completed DPIAs and sharing agreements, or core information about them, accessible to other public sector bodies when it

---

[8] DPIAs show the essential considerations and choices that departments must make when sharing and using specific data.

is appropriate (this reduces duplication of work and means solutions to common challenges can be shared with others).

- Making sure users can easily access nonsensitive or nonpersonal data.

5. *Make data findable, accessible, interoperable, and reusable*:
   - On a practical level, this means using common data standards to make data findable, accessible, interoperable, and reusable across government and regularly engaging with the Data Standards Authority (DSA).

CHAPTER 40

Australian Standards

The National Archives of Australia (National Archives) is considered by many to be a world leader and trendsetter in the field of public sector information governance theory and practice. Its stated purpose is to provide leadership in best-practice management of the official record of the Commonwealth and ensures that Australian government information of enduring significance is secured, preserved, and available to government agencies, researchers, and the community,[1] and in this role, it has developed a series of highly regarded standards, as described in further detail later.

Australian Information Management Legislation

Archives Act, 1983 and Regulations[2]

The Archives Act first sets forth the primary goals and purposes of the National Archives including the obligation to identify which public information has enduring value, the duty to preserve and make public archival material available to the public, and the obligation to promulgate standards and provide data management advice to government agencies.

The Archives Act then describes various critical agency duties including the responsibility to destroy, transfer, or alter government records in a manner that complies with National Archives standards, when Commonwealth archives should be transferred to National Archives, and the obligation to follow various records management requirements.

The Archives Act is supplemented by various regulations which require, among other items, that government agencies keep written

---

[1] Information and data governance framework | naa.gov.au.
[2] Information management legislation | naa.gov.au.

information pertaining to their destruction and transfer of records as well as regarding any alteration or destruction of such records.

An additional order, known as the Senate Continuing Order for the production of departmental and agency file lists, aims to create additional government data transparency by requiring government agencies to publish lists of particular files created in a given six-month period (such as policies, legislative development, and public administrative matters—but not internal administrative documentation) by tabling those files in the Senate and updating their website language.

Additional Legislation and Regulations That Support Defensible Information Governance[3]

In addition to the core data governance standards focused earlier, like most other developed jurisdictions, information governance and privacy standards are "sprinkled" throughout Australia's legislative landscape. Relevant standards include:

- The Public Governance, Performance and Accountability Act 2013, administered by the Department of Finance, which governs how Commonwealth entities utilize public resources and obligates those entities to use information properly and to keep records documenting that use.
- The Commonwealth Procurement Rules, also administered by the Department of Finance, which requires government entities to keep documentation related to the procurement of goods and services in accordance with the Archives Act and protect the confidentiality of information.
- The Crimes Act of 1914, which criminalizes the destruction or created inaccessibility of judicial evidence, the impermissible disclosure of information related to a person's public duties, or the unauthorized disclosure of official secrets.
- The Freedom of Information Act, 1982, which functions similarly to similar laws in other countries and obligates

---

[3] Id.

agencies to publish their information publication scheme including which information they propose to publish and how and to whom they publish that information, and, specifically, to publish 10 categories of information including the agency's structure, functions, operational data, citizen engagement arrangements, and a disclosure log registering information released in response to Freedom of Information (FOI) requests.

- The Privacy Act 1988, Privacy Regulation 2013, and additional legally binding guidelines and rules, administered by the Attorney General's Office and the Office of the Australian Information Commissioner, which governs the collection, usage, storage, and disclosure of personal information; includes specific requirements pertaining to tax ID numbers, medical data, and credit information; and requires agencies to, among other obligations, destroy or de-identify personal information when no longer needed and keep personal information accurate and updated.
- The Fair Work Act and Fair Work Regulations of 2009, administered by the Department of Employment, which mandate employers, including government entities, to allow employees to inspect records that pertain to them, allow employees to make copies of such records, keep legible copies of employee records available for government inspection, help employees to access their records, and ensure that all employee records are kept accurate.
- The Electronic Transactions Act of 1999 and the Electronic Transaction Regulations of 2000, which, respectively, set forth standards for protecting the production, retention, integrity, and copyright of electronic transaction data and describe how to transmit documents electronically (including mandating that documents sent by e-mail must be in a printable and preservable format).

Conclusion

In an era of increasing digitalization, specialization, privacy-consciousness, and connectivity, librarians face the critical responsibility of managing and protecting information resources effectively. Our goal in *A Librarian's Guide to ISO Information Governance Standards, Privacy, and Security* was to provide librarians with some of the critical tools to excel in this crucial role so that they can fulfill their functions and responsibilities as stewards of knowledge in a manner that protects patron privacy, engages staff at all levels, lowers their institutional risk, and avoids the waste of valuable resources.

Throughout this guide, we have explored the significance of adhering to ISO information governance standards, with a specific focus on privacy and security. By embracing internationally recognized standards such as ISO/IEC 15489, ISO 27001, and ISO/IEC 27701 together with best practices for information governance, librarians can fulfill their responsibilities to both their patrons and institutions, using robust and open information security management systems and privacy frameworks.

Understanding and implementing ISO standards in the context of best practices for information governance enables librarians to conduct risk assessments, develop comprehensive information security policies, and integrate privacy and records management considerations into their daily practices. This, in turn, allows librarians to take a proactive approach to information management that includes both the frameworks of Privacy by Design and information governance by design.

The end result of this process will be, we believe, the establishment of a proactive culture of security and privacy awareness within their organizations, which will allow them to safeguard and promote access to valuable information while, at the same time, protecting the rights of individuals. And the first step in this process is to understand which laws, regulations, and standards apply.

About the Authors

Phyllis L. Elin is an Information Governance leader with over 30 years of experience, leading consulting assignments and managing projects for enterprise clients in financial services, pharmaceutical, manufacturing, health care, legal, higher education, and public sector. Currently, Phyllis is the CEO of Knowledge Preservation, an information governance consulting practice based in New Jersey.

Her past consulting projects include integration work related to active file management, development of records retention schedules, creation of policy and procedures manuals, technology solutions, facilities management, hoteling and telecommuting projects, record center administration, vital records and archival records management, vendor evaluations, development of request for informations (RFIs) and request for proposals (RFPs), marketing programs, staff training, and in-house seminars.

Phyllis has taught Library, Records, and Information Governance sessions at Simmons College, Suffolk University, the American Management Association, the Boston Computer Society, and the Association of Legal Administrators, in addition to ARMA International and local ARMA chapter events.

Phyllis is also the author of two related books on information governance: *A Corporate Librarian's Guide to Information Governance and Privacy* and *A Government Librarian's Guide to Information Governance and Privacy*.

Max Rapaport is an Information Governance and data privacy attorney with significant experience managing large-scale legal research and compliance projects within highly regulated industries.

Max is currently the COO of Knowledge Preservation and holds a BA from Cornell University, a JD from the Boston University School of Law, and an LLM from the Georgetown University Law Center. Max co-wrote *A Government Librarian's Guide to Information Governance and Privacy* with Phyllis Elin.

Index

OTHER TITLES IN THE BUSINESS LAW AND CORPORATE RISK MANAGEMENT COLLECTION

- *Mobilizing the C-Suite* by Frank Riccardi
- *Enhanced Enterprise Risk Management* by John Sidwell and Peter Hlavnicka
- *A Corporate Librarian's Guide to Information Governance and Data Privacy* by Phyllis L. Elin
- *A Government Librarian's Guide to Information Governance and Data Privacy* by Phyllis Elin and Max Rapaport
- *Protecting the Brand, Volume II* by Peter Hlavnicka and Anthony M. Keats
- *Can. Trust. Will.* by Leeza Garber and Scott Olson
- *Protecting the Brand, Volume I* by Peter Hlavnicka and Anthony M. Keats
- *Business Sustainability* by Zabihollah Rezaee
- *Business Sustainability Factors of Performance, Risk, and Disclosure* by Zabihollah Rezaee
- *The Gig Mafia* by David M. Shapiro
- *Guerrilla Warfare in the Corporate Jungle* by K. F. Dochartaigh
- *Consumer Protection in E-Retailing in ASEAN* by Huong Ha
- *A Book About Blockchain* by Rajat Rajbhandari
- *Successful Cybersecurity Professionals* by Steven Brown

Concise and Applied Business Books

The Collection listed above is one of 30 business subject collections that Business Expert Press has grown to make BEP a premiere publisher of print and digital books. Our concise and applied books are for...

- Professionals and Practitioners
- Faculty who adopt our books for courses
- Librarians who know that BEP's Digital Libraries are a unique way to offer students ebooks to download, not restricted with any digital rights management
- Executive Training Course Leaders
- Business Seminar Organizers

Business Expert Press books are for anyone who needs to dig deeper on business ideas, goals, and solutions to everyday problems. Whether one print book, one ebook, or buying a digital library of 110 ebooks, we remain the affordable and smart way to be business smart. For more information, please visit www.businessexpertpress.com, or contact sales@businessexpertpress.com.

www.ingramcontent.com/pod-product-compliance
Lightning Source LLC
Chambersburg PA
CBHW061142220326
41599CB00025B/4328